Fort Harker

The name of Fort Ellsworth was changed to Fort Harker, November 17, 1866, to honor Charles Garrison Harker, brigadier general of volunteers, killed June 27, 1864, at the battle of Kenesaw Mountain, Georgia. Born in Swedesborough, New Jersey, December 2, 1837, he graduated from the U.S. Military Academy at West Point in 1858. He first served as brevet second lieutenant, Second U.S. Infantry, July 1, 1858, became second lieutenant, Ninth U.S. Infantry, August 15, 1858, and was promoted to first lieutenant, Fifteenth U.S. Infantry, May 14, 1861. He was promoted to captain October 24, 1861, and became colonel of the Sixty-fifth Ohio Volunteers, November 11, 1861. He fought in the battle of Shiloh, the siege of Corinth, and the battle of Stone River and was recommended for promotion but did not receive it until he had further distinguished himself at Chickamauga and Chattanooga. Named brigadier general of volunteers, September 20, 1863, he commanded a brigade under General Oliver O. Howard in the campaign in Georgia and held the peak of Rocky Face Ridge, May 7, 1864, against the enemy's determined efforts to dislodge him. He died at Kenesaw Mountain when he was twenty-six years old.

Fort Harker
Defending the Journey West

by Leo E. Oliva

Kansas State Historical Society
Topeka, Kansas

THE AUTHOR: Dr. Leo E. Oliva is a former university professor of history. He farms with his wife, Bonita, in Rooks County, Kansas, and is the owner of Western Books publishing company. In addition Oliva is a free-lance historian whose writing and research has focused on the frontier army and Indians as well as local history. *Fort Harker* is his sixth book in the Kansas Forts Series. Oliva's other publications include *Soldiers on the Santa Fe Trail* (1967), *Ash Rock and the Stone Church: The History of a Kansas Rural Community* (1983), and *Fort Union and the Frontier Army in the Southwest* (1993).

FRONT COVER: *Sounding the Call*, Fort Harker, Kansas, 1866–1873, by Jerry D. Thomas. Thomas, a nationally acclaimed artist, has made a career of creating wildlife and western art. His original works will appear on the covers of all eight volumes of the Kansas Forts Series. Thomas is a resident of Manhattan, Kansas.

Fort Harker: Defending the Journey West is the seventh volume in the Kansas Forts Series published by the Kansas State Historical Society in cooperation with the Kansas Forts Network.

Additional Works in the Kansas Forts Series:
Fort Scott: Courage and Conflict on the Border
Fort Hays: Keeping Peace on the Plains
Fort Larned: Guardian of the Santa Fe Trail
Fort Wallace: Sentinel on the Smoky Hill Trail
Fort Dodge: Sentry of the Western Plains
Fort Riley: Citadel of the Frontier West

Library of Congress Card Catalog Number 00-131094

ISBN 0-87726-051-6

Printed by Mennonite Press, Inc., Newton, Kansas

CONTENTS

FOREWORD

Of all the Kansas forts that played a significant role in the history of Kansas, Fort Harker has received the least attention. Leo Oliva's *Fort Harker* provides the first book-length history of this important Kansas military post. Dr. Oliva's monograph is an admirable study that brings to life this frontier fort, which was located near the center of the state and provided a vital link in supplying military operations on the Plains.

First established as Fort Ellsworth in 1864 at the juncture of the Smoky Hill River and the Fort Riley–Fort Larned Road on the Smoky Hill Trail, the post was moved away from the river and renamed Fort Harker in November 1866. The army closed Fort Harker in 1873 after its purpose had been fulfilled. Frontier posts such as Fort Harker were designed to provide an army presence during the construction of the railroad through Kansas and preserve peace on the frontier. In fact, the role became that of subduing the native tribes of the Plains and fostering settlement of the region by Euro-Americans. The critical year in the history of Fort Harker was 1867 when the Plains tribes engaged in warfare to resist the construction of the Kansas Pacific Railroad through Kansas and curb further encroachment of whites into their prime hunting grounds in western Kansas.

In addition to chronicling the activities of the military in relation to the fort, Dr. Oliva presents the social history that unveils the "real" conditions of life in a frontier fort. Descriptions of early Fort Ellsworth are revealing of the difficulties faced by soldiers and their dependents. One of the devastating intrusions on life at the fort and in the civilian population near the fort was the cholera epidemic of 1867.

Dr. Oliva's *Fort Harker* fills a major void in the history of forts in Kansas. Readers will find in this work a new chapter in western forts history that blends the best of military and social history.

Ramon Powers
Executive Director
Kansas State Historical Society

Introduction

Fort Harker, established as Fort Ellsworth in August 1864 on the north side of the Smoky Hill River at the juncture of the Fort Riley–Fort Larned Road and the Smoky Hill Trail, was founded to counter Indian resistance in the region and help forward supplies to military posts farther west. It also served as command headquarters for the District of the Upper Arkansas.

Soldiers stationed at this strategic position on the overland trails, in cooperation with troops from other forts, helped protect wagon trains, stagecoaches, and other travelers through lands claimed by Plains tribes, safeguarding the Fort Riley–Fort Larned Road and portions of the Smoky Hill and Santa Fe Trails. The soldiers also protected railroads, during and after construction, and early settlements in the region.

Fort Harker served briefly as a supply depot, an intermediate post in the Kansas forts network. It was a link in the supply lines between Forts Leavenworth and Riley to the east and Forts Zarah, Larned, Dodge, Hays, and Wallace to the west. It performed an important role in an era of rapid transition from overland trails to railroads and from Indian frontier to settled land. Within a few years Fort Harker fulfilled its assignments. It kept the peace and protected the overland routes of travel, provided a vital supply depot until the railroad built farther west, and served as the command headquarters for the military district. No major battles were fought within its jurisdiction.

By 1867 Fort Harker embodied a four-company garrison, quartermaster supply depot, and command center, with more than seventy-five buildings. During 1867 it was one of the most active forts in Kansas, when scores of wagon trains carried provisions from the supply depot to troops in the field and to forts in western Kansas, eastern Colorado Territory, and New Mexico Territory. The post garrison furnished escorts for most of those wagon trains. The troops stationed there performed more escort duty in 1867 than those stationed at any other frontier post during the post-Civil War era. The post declined in importance after 1868 when the railroad and the scene of most hostilities moved west.

During its brief existence, less than decade, Fort Harker's garrison contributed significantly to the army's role in westward expansion. In addition to escort duty, protection of stage stations, defense of railroad construction crews and railroad stations, and safeguarding frontier settlements, the soldiers at Fort Harker performed usual garrison duties, including construction and maintenance of buildings, guard duty,

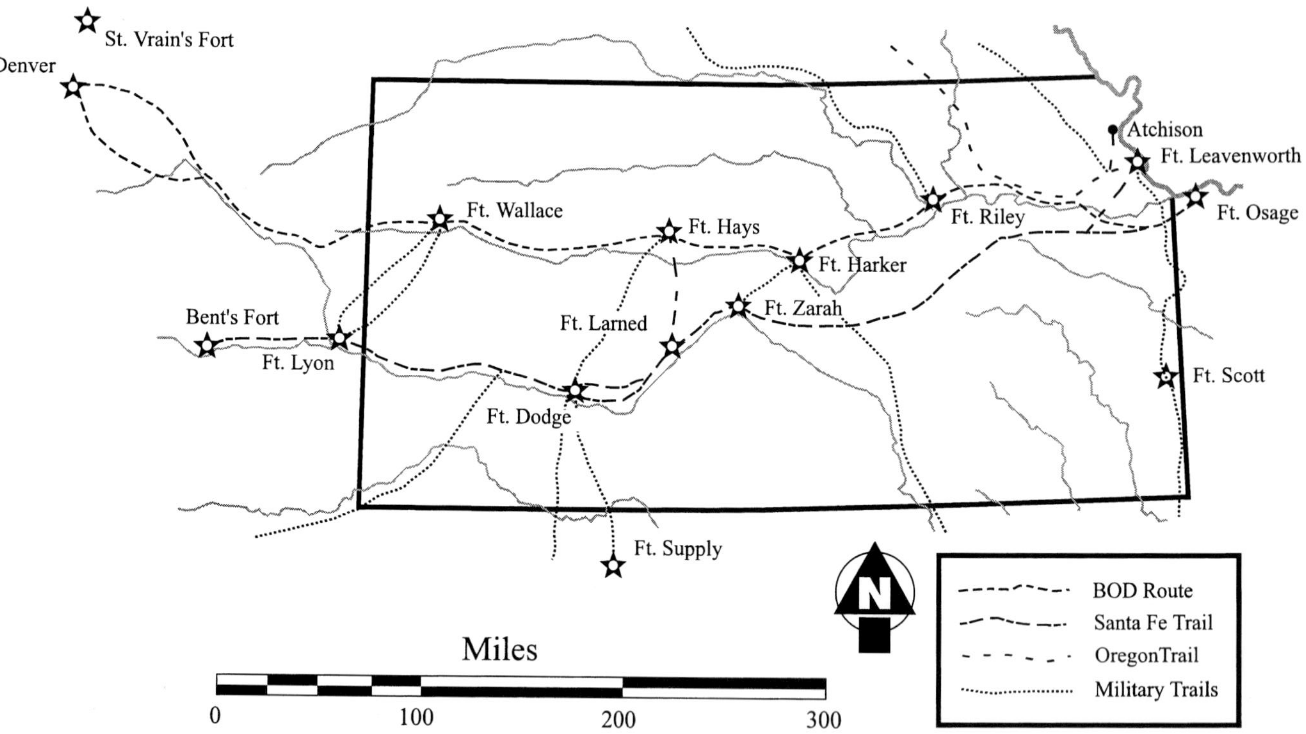

The Kansas forts network, 1870.

policing the grounds, and practicing military maneuvers. When hostilities erupted in the region, soldiers went into the field to attempt to restore peace and punish offenders. The ultimate goal of the army in Kansas was removal of the Indians from the area so Euro-American settlers could occupy and develop the land. This was accomplished by the early 1870s.

Most frontier posts were closed within a few years after the Indians were forced to leave the area. The army closed Fort Harker in 1873 because its purposes had been fulfilled. Later the town of Kanopolis grew around the old post, utilizing some of the structures. A few of those buildings remain today. The story of Fort Harker is part of the saga of Indian–white relations on the Great Plains and the frontier army in Kansas.

1

The U.S. Army

The United States Army was an important part of federal assistance to westward expansion. After the establishment of the United States following the American Revolution, the army protected frontier settlers and routes of travel from American Indians, who objected to the invasion of their lands. The emigrants, when they met Indian opposition, requested protection from the federal government. The government often responded with military aid.

Except during eras of foreign wars or the tragic Civil War, the army was small and poorly funded. Even so, it constructed a line of military posts along the routes of travel and in areas of frontier settlement. From those strongholds troops ventured forth as needed to face real or imagined Indian hostilities and protect Indians from belligerent citizens. Most of the soldiers' efforts were designed to keep the peace, prevent outrages by settlers or Indians, and punish offenders. This occasionally led to warfare, although most encounters were minor skirmishes. A few larger battles erupted, most of which were inconclusive. The army alone did not defeat the Indians nor force them into submission. Rather a combination of circumstances made it impossible for the Indians to maintain their traditional way of life. The army, in concert with railroads, buffalo hunters, and settlers, eventually forced the Indians from their homelands.

The army was only part of federal policy in Indian–white relations. Congress, the Bureau of Indian Affairs, and special agents negotiated

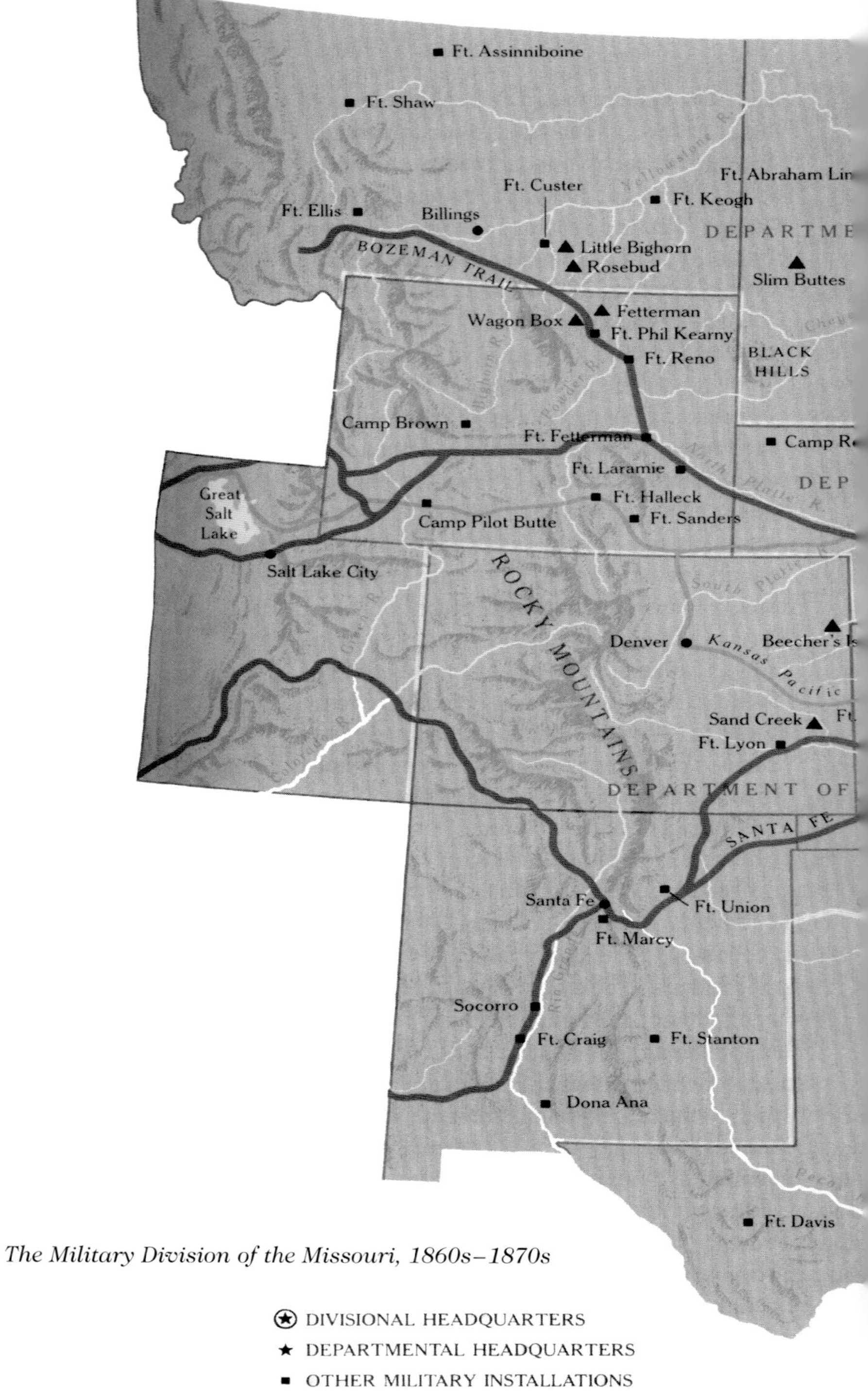

The Military Division of the Missouri, 1860s–1870s

Northern Pacific Railroad
 on
ck
ice
AKOTA
Ft. Sully
dall
St. Paul (HQ)
Chicago
T OF THE PLATTE
Railroad
Pacific
Platte R.
a R.
Omaha (HQ)
Ft. Leavenworth (HQ)
Independence
St. Louis
Kansas R.
Ft. Hays
Ft. Riley
Jefferson Barracks
wner's
tion
Ft. Larned
Ft. Harker
Ft. Dodge
MISSOURI
Camp Supply
Arkansas R.
Washita
Washita R.
Ft. Sill
Red R.
Ft. Richardson
ARTMENT OF TEXAS
olorado R.
Austin
n Antonio (HQ)
Ft. Clark
0   MILES   300

In an effort to end the so-called "Indian problem," the government, with the help of the U.S. Army, made treaties with native tribes to induce them to surrender their lands for white settlement. This J. Howland illustration of the October 1867 treaty at Medicine Lodge Creek appeared in Harper's Weekly, *November 16, 1867.*

settlements with Indian tribes, especially to induce them to surrender lands for white use and settlement. In return the government usually provided other lands that typically were smaller in size and farther from Euro-American settlements. Through combined efforts of Indian treaties and frontier defense, including military posts, the national government contributed significantly to the country's westward expansion.

During and after the Civil War the federal army, assisted occasionally by state volunteer units, faced the difficult task of protecting settlers and routes of travel, subduing Indians considered to be hostile, and opening tribal lands for permanent white settlement. The mission was encumbered by assertive citizens who demanded protection wherever they went, militant journalists and pundits who wanted the Indians annihilated, and a Congress that expected results but failed to appropriate sufficient funds. The army was chronically shorthanded and

Soldiering was not a popular profession as troops endured low pay, poor living conditions, and hard work. This sketch by Private C.C. Chrisman depicts the typical life of a soldier: 1. drill, 2. kitchen duty, 3. cleanup, 4. construction detail, 5. guard duty, 6. punishment.

inadequately equipped for the assignment. In spite of these impediments, the military served as a stabilizing and moderating force in the settling of the continent and helped resolve the nation's so-called "Indian problem."

The army continued to labor under several obstacles. Soldiering was not a popular profession, and the ranks were predominately filled with recent immigrants and unemployed laborers. It was hard to find recruits willing to serve five years and more difficult to retain them. They endured low pay (sixteen dollars per month at the end of the Civil War, reduced to thirteen dollars in 1870), bad living conditions, and severe discipline. Soldiers spent much time at hard labor and standing guard. The provisions, clothing, and equipment left over from the Civil War, regardless of condition, were utilized by the army for the next decade. Drunkenness was a chronic problem among officers and enlisted men, and approximately 25 percent of army personnel were considered to be alcoholics. Desertion was a perennial problem, with losses ranging from 10 percent to 20 percent per year for the entire army.

Federal policy toward Indians was confounding because authority over Indian affairs was divided between the U.S. Army in the War Department and the Bureau of Indian Affairs in the Department of the Interior. Both soldiers and Indians were perplexed as government policy alternated between the use of force and efforts at peaceful negotiations. Periodically peace councils were conducted and treaties were signed. During those times the army was held in check until hostilities broke out again. Keeping the peace was sometimes impossible, given the conflict of cultures and the contest for land, and challenged officers' and soldiers' best efforts.

Although called forts, nearly all military posts on the Plains were not true fortifications. Most, including Fort Harker, had no protecting walls. Some posts had buildings designed for defense, but most were comparable to a small village. Kansas forts comprised officers' quarters, soldiers' barracks, laundresses' quarters, storehouses, repair shops, stables, hospital, outhouses, and a post trader's store grouped around a parade ground. From these bases of operation and supply, the army challenged the Plains Indians.

2

Plains Indians

Fort Harker and the other military posts on the Plains existed because Indians resisted Euro-American invasion of their homelands and hunting grounds. The tribes in Kansas, although few in number and technologically deficient in comparison to the emigrants and the U.S. Army, refused to surrender their lands and traditional ways of life without a fight.

Several tribes resided in or hunted buffalo in central and western Kansas. Kansa Indians lived on a reservation near Council Grove but periodically hunted farther west and occasionally became involved in conflicts with other tribes. Osages from eastern Kansas and present Oklahoma also hunted in western Kansas. Pawnees, who lived in present Nebraska and northern Kansas, came south to hunt and raid along overland routes. They usually were as threatening to other tribes in the area as to Euro-Americans.

The southern bands of the Cheyenne and Arapaho tribes were located north of the Arkansas River in present western Kansas and eastern Colorado. Some of the Lakota Sioux from the Northern Plains periodically came into the same region to hunt. Comanches, Kiowas, and Plains Apaches (also called Kiowa Apaches because of their close alliance with the Kiowas), resided mainly to the south of the Arkansas but traveled north of the river to hunt and raid.

Tribal populations were not large in the nineteenth century, especially compared with the growing United States. The many bands of

7

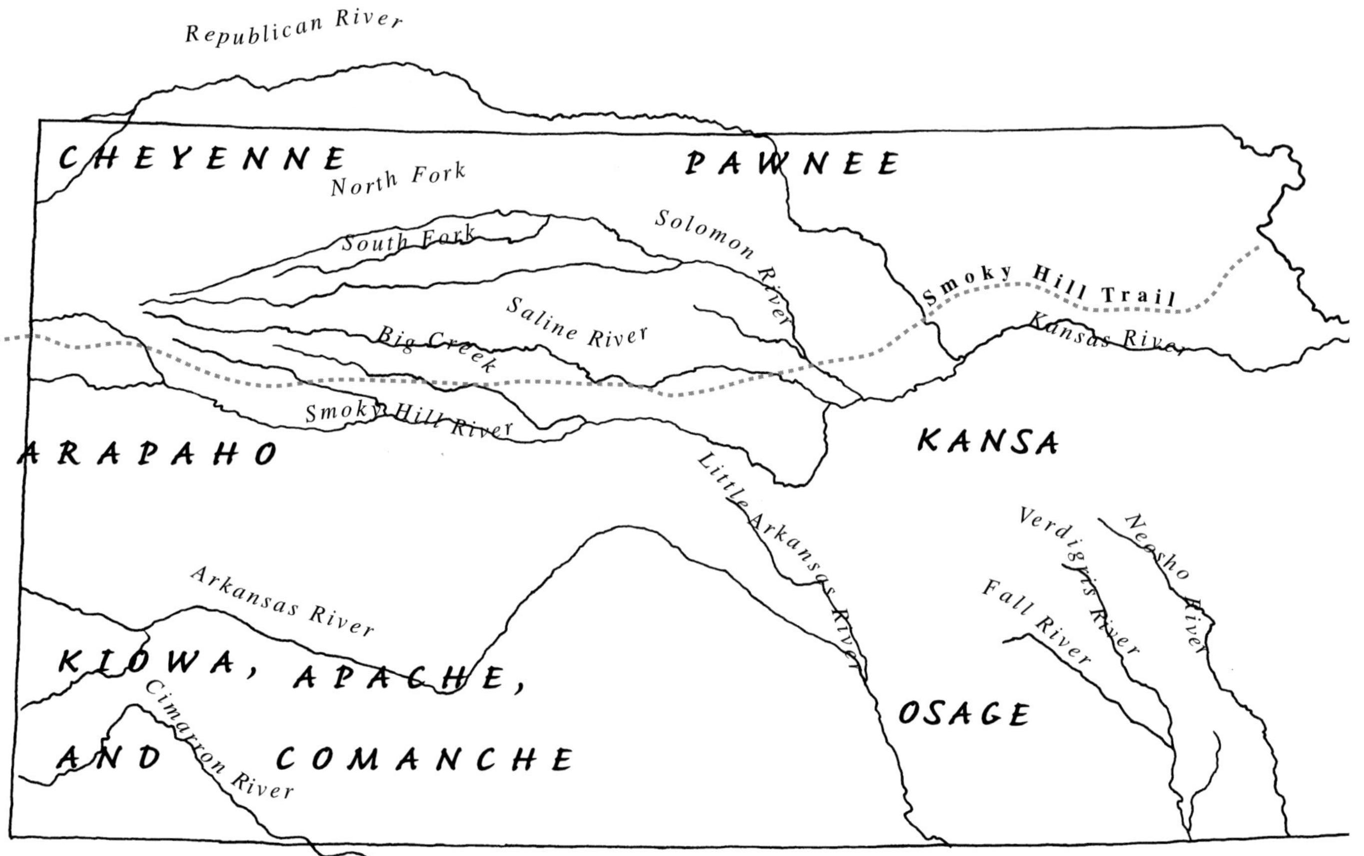

Location of Indian tribes in Kansas, ca. 1870.

The great buffalo herds, vital to the Indians' existence, were depleted by encroaching white settlement across the Plains. When Indians resisted Euro-American intruders, they were not only protecting their homelands, they were fighting for the survival of their entire way of life. This painting entitled A Buffalo Hunt on the Southwestern Prairies *is by artist/explorer John Mix Stanley.*

Sioux, most of whom were on the Northern Plains, created the largest of these groups with about twenty thousand people. Only a few hundred of these came regularly to the area of present western Kansas. Other populations numbered approximately 6,000 Osages, 1,500 Kansas, 10,000 Pawnees, 7,000 Comanches, 2,000 Kiowas, 300 Plains or Kiowa Apaches, 3,500 Cheyennes, and 3,000 Arapahos.

These tribes hunted near the Santa Fe and Smoky Hill Trails, and some came to the trails to raid wagon trains, particularly those that were small or not well protected. Later, when the Indians saw their continued life on the Plains seriously threatened by the intruders, some Cheyennes, Arapahos, Comanches, and Kiowas fought back with a vengeance.

The Indians defended their families, economic base, and culture. The Euro-Americans, on the other hand, viewed Indian resistance as thievery, savagery, and murder. The Indians held similar views of the intruders. Neither side understood nor appreciated the culture of the other, making accommodation virtually impossible as long as the Indians

Little Robe, Southern Cheyenne chief

Kicking Bird, Kiowa chief

held land the Euro-Americans wanted. Under these circumstances, conflict was probably unavoidable. Given the relative population and technology, the outcome was inevitable. The result, however, was the loss of substantial property and lives on both sides.

The buffalo–horse culture of the Plains tribes was a recent development in the long history of people known as Indians, whose ancestors had migrated to North America thousands of years ago. A succession of cultures had periodically occupied the Great Plains. As some groups migrated from other regions, they pushed out those who had come before. Thus the tribes found on the Plains in the nineteenth century had not been there long, and some of them arrived on the scene about the same time as did the Euro-Americans, who were the last to claim the country successfully.

These tribal Americans hunted buffalo throughout the region and encamped along the Arkansas, Smoky Hill, and other rivers and their tributaries. Some places were considered sacred and utilized for religious ceremonies. When they resisted Euro-American intruders into their territories, the Indians were not only protecting their homeland, they were fighting for the survival of their entire way of life.

Warfare, particularly raiding and stealing horses, was a central feature of Plains cultures. Courage and bravery in battle became the highest virtues, and from an early age men were trained to fight as well as

Yellow Bear, Arapaho chief

hunt. They were considered by many observers to be the world's finest horsemen, and they developed well the skill of hit-and-run raiding and the decoy-ambush tactic. They were prepared to resist outsiders who penetrated their hunting grounds, especially since they were familiar with the terrain. They were defeated, however, by superior technology and overwhelming numbers.

Gradually some tribes became allies. Kiowas and Comanches shared some of the same territory and stopped fighting each other, especially after Euro-American penetration of the Plains increased. Cheyennes and Arapahos were allies before they reached the Central Plains, and eventually they worked out accommodations with Kiowas and Comanches. Pawnees, on the other hand, considered all other tribes in the region to be their enemies. Cheyennes fought against the Kansas. Combined, the Plains tribes could have provided a formidable resistance, but they never united in opposition to the Euro-Americans. The army frequently had Indian allies, particularly Indian scouts in its military operations against specific tribes.

Tribal resistance to Euro-American encroachment on their lands developed slowly until the war between the United States and Mexico (1846–1848), during which time Indian attacks on overland travelers increased dramatically. It was apparently at this time that the Plains tribes realized how much their economic base and way of life was threatened by the increasing numbers of Euro-Americans. These intruders

Besieged on all sides by white settlement, the military, and economic interests such as the railroad, Indians of Kansas faced an uncertain future. In this illustration, published in Harper's Weekly, *May 10, 1873, an Indian spokesman presents his concerns.*

threatened the Indians' space and culture, brought fatal diseases such as smallpox and cholera, introduced trade items on which the Indians became dependent, and brought whiskey, which contributed to the disruption of native society and, sometimes, Indian–white relations.

Tensions further increased with the gold rush to California, beginning in 1849. Large areas of Indian lands were still undisturbed by people from the United States crossing the Plains, leaving many safe havens for the native population. Indian resistance increased, however, as some native leaders perceived a greater threat to follow. That came with the Colorado gold rush in 1858 and after, which launched the final contest for control of the Plains, eliminating all sanctuaries for the Indians. The onrush of settlers, opening of new trails through Indian lands, destruction of resources, and renewed efforts to force the Indians from the Central Plains combined to force the Plains tribes to retreat to reservations or fight for their lands. The struggle for control of the Plains intensified during and after the Civil War. Fort Ellsworth/Harker became part of that contest in 1864. It began as a small military encampment established to help protect travelers on the overland trails.

3

Overland Trails

The Santa Fe Trail (1821–1880), oldest trail across the Plains, connected the Missouri River valley with New Mexico. It was a commercial road linking two nations until 1848, when a large portion of northern Mexico was attached to the United States. Military protection for this route was provided occasionally by escorts for wagon trains, beginning in 1829, and the establishment of military posts, including Fort Mann near present Dodge City, Kansas (1846–1848); Fort Atkinson (1850–1854) near the site of Fort Mann; Fort Union, New Mexico (1851–1891); Fort Larned, Kansas (1859–1878); and Fort Lyon, Colorado (1860–1889). Other military posts in Kansas, although not situated on the Santa Fe Trail, helped provide periodic protection: Fort Leavenworth (1829–present), Fort Scott (1843–1852), and Fort Riley (1853–present).

Soon after Fort Riley became the primary base for men and supplies serving on the frontier of Kansas Territory, a military road was opened from that post to join the Santa Fe Trail near Walnut Creek crossing (east of present Great Bend, Kansas). The army constructed a bridge over the Smoky Hill River on this route in 1857 to facilitate the transport of military supplies. A flood destroyed a bridge the following year, but the army and civilian freighters continued to use this route.

After Fort Larned was established near the crossing of Pawnee Fork in 1859, the road from Fort Riley, known as the Fort Riley–Fort Larned Road, assumed increased importance. Military personnel and freight

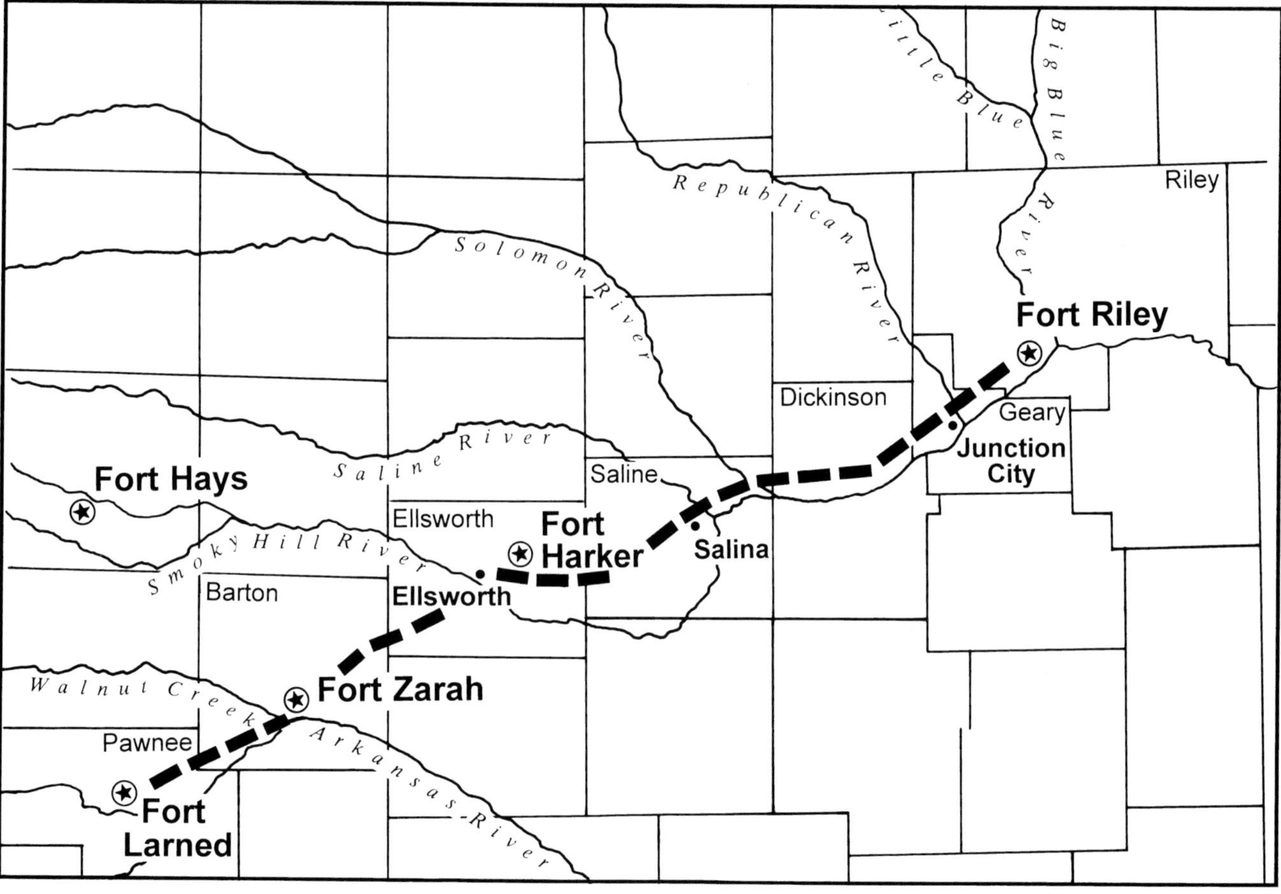

The Fort Riley–Fort Larned Road provided a vital connection to the western part of the state for military personnel, freighters, and stage lines.

Military escorts often were necessary to protect civilian travelers on the Santa Fe and Smoky Hill Trails.

traveled this part of the Santa Fe Trail network. In 1862 the Kansas Stage Company won a contract to deliver mail and operate a stage line between Junction City (near Fort Riley) and Fort Larned. The company made plans to establish stage stations at several places along this road. One of these stations, located at the crossing of the Smoky Hill River, later became the original location for Fort Ellsworth/Harker.

The Smoky Hill Trail, utilized beginning in 1859 to travel from the Missouri River to the gold fields of present Colorado, followed the same route from Fort Riley to the Smoky Hill River crossing, from which point it continued west along the Smoky Hill valley to its headwaters and on to Denver. This trail was the shortest route between the Missouri River and the Rocky Mountain mining camps.

The Smoky Hill River runs nearly six hundred miles from its source in eastern Colorado to its junction with the Republican River at present Junction City, Kansas, to form the Kansas River, an important tributary of the Missouri River at Kansas City. A route along the Smoky Hill valley was well known to the Indians, who followed the water supply and found good hunting among buffalo herds and other game that abounded in the region. The Smoky Hill River was explored in 1844 by John C. Frémont

TABLE OF DISTANCES
FROM
Atchison to the Gold Mines,
VIA THE

First Standard Parallel Route to the Republican Fork of the Kansas River, thence following the trail of Col. Fremont on his explorations in 1843, to Cherry Creek and the Mines.

Compiled from Col. Fremont's Surveys, and the most reliable information derived from the traders across the Great Plains.

FROM ATCHISON TO	MILES.	TOTAL	REMARKS.
Lancaster,	9		Settlement, provisions and grass.
Muscotah, on Grasshopper,	11	20	Settlement, provisions and grass,
Eureka	11	31	Settlement, provisions and grass.
Ontario, on Elk Creek.	10	41	Settlement, provisions and grass.
America, on Soldiers Creek,	9	50	Settlement, provisions and grass.
Vermillion City,	25	75	Settlement, entertainment and provisions.
Crossing of Big Blue,	3	78	Heavy timber and grass.
Little Blue Creek,	17	95	Timber and grass.
Head of do do.	23	118	Wood, water and grass.
Republican Fork.	12	130	Col. Fremont describes this section as "affording
do do Crossing,	2	132	an excellent road, it being generally over high and
Branch of Solomon's Fork,	38	170	level prairies, with numerous streams, which are well
Leaves do do do.	75	245	timbered with ash, elm, and very heavy oak, and
Branch of Republican Fork.	15	260	abounding in herds of buffalo, elk and antelope."
Following up Rep. to its head,	190	450	Heavy timber and grass along the course
Beaver Creek.	23	473	Wood, grass and buffalo.
Bijou Creek,	22	495	Wood, grass and buffalo.
Kioway Creek,	15	510	The route from this point to to the mines runs thro'
Cherry Creek and the Mines,	25	535	a country well timbered and watered, with luxurient grass and plenty of wild game.

ROUTE FROM ATCHISON,
VIA
The Great Military Road to Salt Lake, and Col. Fremont's Route in 1841.

FROM ATCHISON TO	MILES.	TOTAL	REMARKS.
Mormon Grove,	3½		Junction of the Great Military road,
Lancaster,	5½	9	Provisions and grass.
Huron, (crossing Grasshoper,)	4	13	Provisions and grass.
Kennekuk, do main do.	10	23	First Salt Lake Mail Station.
Capioma, (Walnut Creek,)	17	40	Provisions, timber and grass.
Richmond, (head of Nemaha,)	15	55	Provisions, timber and grass.
Marysville,	40	95	Salt Lake Mail Station and provisions.
Small Creek on Prairie,	10	105	Water and grass.
do do.	10	115	Luxurient grass.
do do.	7	122	Water and grass.
Wyth Creek,	7	129	Wood and grass.
Big Sandy Creek,	13	142	Wood and grass.
Dry Sandy Creek,	17	159	Wood and luxurient grass.
Little Blue River,	12	171	Heavy timber.
Road leaves Little Blue,	44	215	Wood and grass.
Small Creek,	7	222	Wood and grass.
Plat e River,	17	239	Wood, grass and buffalo.
Ft. Kearney,	10	249	Salt Lake Mail Station and provisions.
17 Mile Point,	17	266	Wood, water and grass.
Plum Creek,	18	284	Wood and grass.
Cottonwood Spring,	40	324	Wood and grass.
Fremont's Springs,	40	364	Luxurient grass.
O'Failon's Bluffs,	5	369	Wood, water and grass.
Crossing South Platte,	40	409	Wood, water and grass.
Ft. St. Vrain,	200	609	Provisions, and from this to the mines the route is
Cherry Creek,	40	649	well timbered and watered.

ROUTE FROM ATCHISON,
VIA THE
SMOKY HILL FORK ROUTE

FROM ATCHISON TO	MILES.	TOTAL.	REMARKS.
Mormon Grove,	3¼		Junction of the Great Military Road.
Monrovia,	8¾	12	Provisions, entertainment and grass.
Mouth of Bill's Creek,	13	25	On the Grasshopper, Wood and grass.
Ter. Road from Nebraska,	15	40	Wood, water and grass.
Soldier Creek;	10	50	Wood and grass.
Lost Creek,	15	65	Wood and grass,
Louisville.	10	75	Water and grass,
Manhattan City,	12	87	Water, wood and grass.
Ft. Riley,	15	102	Water, wood and grass.
Salina,	52	154	Wood, water and grass.
Pawnee Trail—Smoky Hill,	130	234	Grass and buffalo chips,
Pawnee Fork,	35	319	Grass and buffalo chips.
Arkansas Crossing,	35	354	Wood, water and grass.
Bent's Fort.	150	504	Wood, water and grass.
Bent's Old Fort,	40	544	Water and grass.
Huerfano,	40	584	Water and grass.
Fontaine qui Bouille,	15	599	Wood, water and grass.
Crossing of same,	18	617	Wood, water and grass.
Jim's Camp,	15	632	Water and grass.
Brush Corral,	12	644	Wood, water and grass.
Head of Cherry Creek,	26	670	Wood, water and grass.
Crossing of same,	35	705	From this point to the mines there is heavy timber,
Mines,	6	711	and grass and water in abundance.

Because a military survey party found no Indians along the Smoky Hill Trail, the Butterfield Overland Despatch began operations in 1865. It was immediately beset by Indian opposition.

of the U.S. topographical engineers, but it was not an important trail for United States citizens until the Colorado gold rush of 1859.

Businessmen in towns along the Missouri River promoted the Smoky Hill artery, and several guidebooks were published without benefit of investigating the route. Those who attempted to follow this "trail" discovered it really did not exist except on paper. Some became lost, and others nearly perished. In one party several men starved to death, and there is evidence of cannibalism. The proposed trail along the Smoky Hill fell into disrepute, and some called it the starvation trail. The route needed a thorough exploration.

To assist those using this route, William Green Russell led a thirty-six-man survey team from Leavenworth to Denver early in 1860 to prepare a map and guide to the trail. They reported favorably on the availability of water and grass and noted the presence of wood at some potential campsites. Where firewood was not always available, buffalo chips could be used as fuel. The major obstacle to the use of this route was the presence of Indians. Discounting that warning, the boosters seized upon this favorable report and decided a road should be laid out, camping sites identified, and stream crossings improved.

In June 1860 H. T. Green of Leavenworth conducted a twenty-nine-man survey party over the route, taking time to improve stream crossings and locate some favorable campsites. Green recommended that travelers going to the Colorado mines follow this route, which they would find easy to negotiate and nearly one hundred miles shorter than either the Arkansas or Platte routes. He was unaware of or discounted Indian threats to travelers.

The Civil War interrupted plans for developing this road along the Smoky Hill River, and little was done until 1865, the year after Fort Ellsworth/Harker was founded. With the close of the Civil War, David A. Butterfield, a former Denver businessman who resided in Atchison, Kansas, prepared to open a freight and stagecoach business over the Smoky Hill Trail. Aware of increasing Indian resistance on the Plains, Butterfield requested military assistance.

In June 1865 Major General Grenville M. Dodge, commanding the Department of the Missouri at Fort Leavenworth, sent Second Lieutenant Julian R. Fitch of the U.S. Signal Corps to survey the Smoky Hill route. Lieutenant Fitch led a survey team and construction crew, headed by Isaac E. Eaton, Butterfield's associate, over this route during June, July, and August, to locate and establish stage stations at intervals of approximately twelve miles. The survey was escorted by 250 troops.

This survey party saw no Indians, perhaps because troops were present. Fitch noted the absence of Indians and declared that "the advantages of the Smoky Hill route over the Platte and Arkansas must be apparent to everybody." It was shorter, had more water, timber, buffalo chips, and grass, did not have long stretches of sand to pass through as did the other routes, and had several good places to locate military posts. It was presumed that military protection would be essential for a successful stagecoach operation along the route.

Eaton, who had a stake in this route, was equally impressed with the potential of this trail and declared that "the roadbed itself is the best natural one I have ever seen, and I fail to do the Smoky Hill route justice when I say it is 100 per cent superior to either the Platte or Arkansas routes in every respect." By September 1865 the Butterfield Overland Despatch began operations. It was immediately beset by Indian opposition, similar to that which harried travelers on the Santa Fe Trail during and after the Civil War. Fort Ellsworth/Harker and other Kansas military posts were quickly involved in efforts to protect travel on the Smoky Hill Trail.

4

The Founding of Fort Ellsworth

During the Civil War, as military freighting across the Plains increased to keep supplies flowing to troops in the Southwest, expanded Indian raids necessitated additional protection of the overland routes. The small network of military posts (including Forts Riley and Larned in Kansas, Lyon in Colorado, and Union in New Mexico) could not successfully counter increased Indian attacks along the overland routes.

In 1864 military leaders anticipated a major Indian uprising on the Plains, as war leaders of several tribes saw an opportunity to strike hard while the United States was engaged in civil war. Thus the army made plans to establish new military posts at strategic points on the trails. Within a year the army founded several forts. Fort Ellsworth (later Fort Harker) was one of those posts.

In April 1864 Indian hostilities along the Santa Fe Trail increased, with various wagon trains raided. The following month saw attacks on stage stations and travelers, many of whom asked for protection from the small garrison at Fort Larned. Reinforcements soon arrived, without which the trail may have been closed. In July 1864 war parties attacked various wagon trains, killed several teamsters, and looted wagons. The same month a party of Kiowas stole 172 horses and mules at Fort

In 1864 hostilities along the Santa Fe Trail increased, with wagon trains and stage stations being raided. Because of these continuing problems, military leaders made plans to establish new military posts at strategic points on the trail. This exaggerated drawing of an Indian attack appeared in Harper's Weekly, September 19, 1868.

Larned. A short time later Indians raided wagon trains near Cow Creek, with additional losses.

General Samuel R. Curtis led four hundred troops from Fort Riley to push the Indians away from the Santa Fe Trail and the Fort Riley–Fort Larned Road. On July 28, at Walnut Creek crossing near the point where the road from Fort Riley joined the older, main Santa Fe Trail, Curtis established Fort Zarah, named to honor his son, Major Zarah Curtis, killed in an engagement with William C. Quantrill's guerrillas at Baxter Springs, Kansas, October 6, 1863. Fort Zarah was situated to protect an important stream crossing and to supply troop escorts for freight, stage, and mail service on the Santa Fe Trail.

Soon afterward, Curtis established a military camp, which became Fort Ellsworth, at the Fort Riley–Fort Larned Road crossing of the Smoky Hill River. Both new posts were designed to help guard the trails, keep open the lines of communication, and assure that vital supply trains reached their destinations. Although the expedition caused Indi-

Major General Samuel Ryan Curtis (1807–1866), commanding the Department of Kansas, led a military expedition from Fort Riley during the summer of 1864 to protect overland trails from Indian raids. During that expedition he established Fort Zarah and Fort Ellsworth to help patrol the Fort Riley–Fort Larned Road. The Indians avoided his command, staying clear of the soldiers, but they resumed raiding when Curtis returned to Fort Riley. Curtis graduated from West Point in 1831 and served in the army a short time, resigning to become a civil engineer. He returned to service during the Mexican War as colonel with the Second Ohio Volunteers. He served as representative from Iowa to the U.S. Congress, 1857–1861, resigning to become colonel of the Second Iowa Volunteers. He quickly won promotion to brigadier general of volunteers and, after his victory over Confederate forces at Pea Ridge, Arkansas, March 6–8, 1862, became major general of volunteers. He retired from the army in April 1866 and died a few months later at his home in Iowa.

ans to retreat temporarily (they avoided contact with large military units whenever possible), as soon as Curtis returned to Fort Riley the Cheyennes, Arapahos, Kiowas, and Comanches resumed raiding along the trails. Forts Zarah and Ellsworth helped defend portions of the transportation routes.

Fort Ellsworth occupied a site where a stage station and trading ranch previously had been built. When the Kansas Stage Company began service over the Fort Riley–Fort Larned Road in 1862, the firm established five stage stations: two at the young settlements of Abilene and Salina, and the other three at the crossings of the Smoky Hill River, Cow Creek, and Walnut Creek. A hunting camp and trading ranch, operated

Lieutenant Allen Ellsworth, Seventh Iowa Cavalry, was commander of the military camp that became Fort Ellsworth. He oversaw the construction of a log blockhouse at the new post, and he later claimed the post had been named for his service. Some accepted this view, noting that the name of the post was changed later when Lieutenant Ellsworth was stripped of his commission for some violation of military discipline (details unknown). Newspaper reporter Henry M. Stanley wrote at Fort Harker in April 1867, "It was formerly known by the name of Ellsworth, after an officer of that name. The officer having lost his commission, the fort lost its name, and received the more reputable one of Harker." There is reason to believe, however, that the post was initially named Ellsworth to honor the lieutenant's uncle, Colonel Ephraim Ellsworth, who was killed early in the Civil War.

by Daniel Page and Joseph Lehman (or Lemon), already existed at the Smoky Hill crossing. The two frontiersmen had established their hunting camp in 1860, procuring wolf hides and buffalo hides and tallow for trade. They also engaged in some trade with passing travelers.

On August 1, 1862, the Page and Lehman trading ranch became a station for the Kansas Stage Company. It provided meals for company employees and kept and fed mules that were changed when stagecoaches came through. The two men experienced occasional threats to their safety. The station was raided by Confederate brigands on September 17, 1862, and seventeen mules were stolen. The first recorded Indian menace along this section of the trail occurred nearly two years later.

Colonel Ephraim Elmer Ellsworth (1837–1861), Eleventh New York Infantry, was the first Union officer killed in the Civil War. He was removing a Confederate flag from atop the Marshall House in Alexandria, Virginia, when hotel owner Jim Jackson shot and killed him. A private in Colonel Ellsworth's regiment, Francis Edwin Brownell, shot and killed Jackson. For this Brownell was promoted to the rank of lieutenant and later was awarded a medal of honor. Several sources claim that Fort Ellsworth was named to memorialize the colonel. This seems logical since many frontier posts were named to honor Union officers killed in the Civil War. Also, it was not unusual for military commanders to change the name of a frontier military post. Fort Ellsworth became Fort Harker in 1866.

On May 17, 1864, a Cheyenne war party attacked the stage station at Cow Creek to the southwest and killed one employee. The other two employees escaped and made it to the Smoky Hill, where they warned Page and Lehman and others in the vicinity. Everyone in the nearby area fled to Salina for protection, and Page and Lehman abandoned their trading ranch and stage station.

A few months later, in early August 1864, General Curtis selected the abandoned ranch (a portion of which was still used as a station for the Kansas Stage Company) for a military camp. Second Lieutenant Allen Ellsworth and a portion of Company H, Seventh Iowa Cavalry, were stationed there to erect a blockhouse and temporary quarters. When these troops arrived cannot be determined from available records, but an Indian raiding party captured most of the horses belonging to the soldiers and five mules belonging to the Kansas Stage Company on August 7, 1864. In addition to the log blockhouse was a sod building, twenty-five by forty feet, used as a commissary storehouse. It may have been the stage station and ranch building that Page and Lehman had abandoned.

The soldiers lived in tents until they constructed dugouts along the banks of the Smoky Hill River. Eventually, log structures served as quarters for officers and some of the enlisted men.

On September 17, 1864, Lieutenant Henry W. Garfield, Seventh Iowa Cavalry, arrived and assumed command of the new post, officially named Fort Ellsworth on September 19, 1864. It is not clear for whom the post was named, since the order did not stipulate. Some army officers, especially Lieutenant Allen Ellsworth, and others, including newspaper reporters, later claimed that the post was named to honor Lieutenant Ellsworth for his efforts in the speedy construction of a log blockhouse. Other sources declare it was named to honor Lieutenant Ellsworth's uncle, Colonel Ephraim Elmer Ellsworth, Eleventh New York Infantry, who was the first Union officer killed in the Civil War, May 24, 1861, at Alexandria, Virginia. The fort's name was converted to Harker in November 1866 to honor Brigadier General Charles Garrison Harker killed June 27, 1864, at the battle of Kenesaw Mountain, Georgia. The name of the fort changed, but Ellsworth remained the name of a nearby town and the county organized there in 1867.

Fort Ellsworth/Harker forwarded supplies to the forts farther west, and the garrison performed escort duties. The post became district headquarters with the reorganization of the army after the Civil War. The District of the Upper Arkansas, including western Kansas and eastern Colorado Territory, was one of four districts within the Department of the Missouri (headquartered at Fort Leavenworth), which was one of four departments in the Military Division of the Missouri (headquartered at St. Louis, later Chicago). Fort Ellsworth/Harker, despite its small size and garrison, performed several missions, including district headquarters (command); quartermaster and commissary depot (supply); and base for troops to protect overland trails, railroads, and regional settlements (military operations).

The construction of a new post approximately one mile northeast of the first fort began in the late summer or early autumn of 1866, to place it near the line of the railroad, expected to be completed to this point in 1867. It is possible the planned relocation of the post was the reason for changing the name, which occurred while the new post was under construction but before the move took place. The first Fort Ellsworth/Harker was never an impressive military post according to those who left descriptions of it.

5

Life at the First Fort

Life at the first fort, by all accounts, was austere and unpleasant. The few surviving descriptions by residents provide the only details of conditions there. On December 2, 1865, Lieutenant Ferdinand Edwin de Courcy, Thirteenth U. S. Infantry, commanding the post, told the department commander at Fort Leavenworth that

> the men of this command are suffering very much from Diarrhea and other diseases and as there is no medical officer nor medicines of any kind at this post, I would respectfully request that a medical officer be ordered here to render medical assistance to the men who are really suffering from want of proper treatment.
>
> If a medical officer cannot be ordered here I hope the district Commander will give me authority to hire a citizen Surgeon until such time as a medical officer can be ordered to this post.

The earliest known description of the post was provided by Private John Morrill, a soldier in the Forty-eighth Wisconsin Infantry on his way to serve at Fort Larned. He described Fort Ellsworth as he saw it on September 23, 1865, in a letter to his wife and family:

> We are now in camp at Ft E as it is termed but you would smile to see the Ft. there is a groupe of log shanties covred with dirt. most of the windows are made of boards hung on leather hinges & made to swing open & shut. there is two or three of them which have a half window

25

ARMY LIFE ON THE BORDER.

The romantic side of life in a wild country is generally seen in pictorial newspapers over such pieces as Alice Cary's poem in the Christmas number of *Harper's Weekly*. Such representations bear about the same relation to the dread reality that the Indians of "Hiawatha" do to the sneaking cruel savage of the plain. The kind of people one meets with do not generally belong to the class of romancers, and, though we often read of those peculiarly constituted natures, that can work all day skinning bufla loes and tanning hides, and then read Tennyson aloud in the family circle evenings, they are scarce items in one's real experience.

Travelling on the plains you will generally meet four kinds of people, viz : Indians, Army officers and men, settlers, and roaming hard cases driven by crime to an uncivilized country ; four more entertaining sets of individuals can scarcely be imagined, and if we had any promise of Methuselah's longevity, we wouldn't grudge a year or two spent in sight-seeing between the Mississippi and Rocky Mountains, but life is too short for us to thoroughly enjoy a separation from all comforts and nearly all necessaries. Any little Xantippe expressions in our view of Kansas will be chargeable therefore to the brevity of human existence. Horace Walpole used to say, that the further he travelled the less he wondered at anything ; the further we travel, the more we wonder how anybody who has lived in the shadow of Faneuil Hall ever moved out of it !

Fort Harker, where we at present dwell, is twenty miles from the centre of the United States ; if it were twenty miles from the centre of the earth it would be quite as useful. It has been an established post for two years, but those two years have failed to rear a single comfortable habitation for man, to say nothing about the hundreds of horses and mules that have stood all Winter shelterless.

Our own dwelling, twelve feet square, is made of rough logs, set upright and plastered with mud ; the roof is a heterogeneous mass of mud, sticks, straw and boughs. The former, owing to its profound respect for the law of gravitation, would persist, at first, in falling in clods at all hours. It dropped upon our plates at dinner and into our mouth in dreams, till finally, a bright idea striking us, we stretched a piece of tent cloth above our bed and defied the mud. It snowed the night of our experiment, and a bushel or so of snow sifted into the tent cloth. Toward morning came a thaw. We were dreaming ourselves a victim of the Spanish Inquisition, and they were trying on us the torture of the shaven head and ice-cold drops of water. Just as we were about to renounce Protestanism in toto, we were awakened to a sense of the reality. The water was dripping from our cotton roof in quarts, and, as we wrung ourselves out, a few clods of mud fell with a loud thump, in the opposite corner, as if to remind us that in an uncivilized country man can never war successfully with the elements

A correspondent (apparently a soldier) for the Boston Transcript described Fort Harker (still at the first site) in January 1867. His article, "Army Life on the Border," was published in the February 16, 1867, issue of the Army and Navy Journal. Reprinted here is a portion of that piece.

sash & some of them two or more lights of glass in them. I suppose the aristocracy reside in them which have the glass. it is a military post there are soldiers established here. there is but verry few log shakes [shacks] perhaps 8 or ten in all & a cat could go in & out of them between the logs. there is a row of caves along the river bank in which the Soldiers burrow in winter.

Morrill was not impressed with the country either, as he wrote from Fort Zarah on September 26, 1865, after traveling from Fort Ellsworth:

there is thousands & thousands of acres with not a bush on [them?] on the streams most of them there is some timber. some has none & the others have but little. The one we camped on yesterday had none. This country should be left to the Indians & Wild beasts & such is pretty much the case. there is not a human habitation between here & where I last wrote, & here & there they do not look as though human beings should inhabit them.

The post commander, Captain John Green, Second U.S. Cavalry, described Fort Ellsworth in a letter to department headquarters, February 7, 1866:

The Garrison at present consists of two (2) Companies, one (1) of Infantry, and one (1) of Cavalry.

The Post is entirely destitute of a Stable, the Horses are only Sheltered from the weather, by a mass of brush and dirt, that was thrown up temporarily for that purpose, this was erected by 1st Lieut C. H. Lester 2nd U.S. Cavalry, in the early part of the winter, and was the best that could be built with the material on hand at the time.

The Post is also destitute of a Store Room for Quartermaster and Commissary Stores, and much damage is sustained by the Government, upon that account.

The Officers on duty at the Post (three in number) are living in three small huts.

The Quarters occupied by the enlisted men, consist of a poor set of log huts, nearly all of them without windows, and so low that a man can scarcely stand upright in them, without floors, and are much in need of repair.

I would therefore respectfully recommend, that material and mechanics be furnished, to put this post in a proper state of repair.

Not only were the buildings inadequate and uncomfortable, the quartermaster and commissary stores at the post in April 1866, described by the post commander, Captain Kilburn Knox, Thirteenth U.S. Infantry, were "in a most miserable state, and over three fourths of them totally unfit for issue." The same month fires destroyed all the hay at the post, leaving the livestock dependent on grazing for sustenance.

On April 16 Captain Knox declared that the old quarters were nearly uninhabitable, and he requested new buildings for the post. He had a long list of buildings because everything at the post was in need of replacement. In some cases, such as stables and storehouses, none had yet been built. New construction did not begin until several months later.

When the guardhouse at the original Fort Ellsworth/Harker location was completely destroyed by fire on January 29, 1867, some of the soldiers must have thought it was the proper disposal of a wretched building. Some may have wished other buildings, including quarters, would meet the same end because their destruction might hasten the construction of the new post. Officers' wives also found the post a miserable place.

Alice Blackwood Baldwin, young bride of Lieutenant Frank D. Baldwin, Thirty-seventh U.S. Infantry, arrived at the original Fort Ellsworth/Harker site in 1867, shortly after their marriage. They reached the post in a snow storm on January 30, the day after the guardhouse burned. The crude fort was a shock to Mrs. Baldwin. She described her experiences:

> Eager and happy to be at last at the end of a long day's journey, I looked but could see nothing through the thick snow which had been falling all day. I could see no buildings nor any sign of a "fort" until it was pointed out to me, but still could see nothing but a spot elevated slightly above the rest of the landscape. A nearer approach disclosed a short stub of stovepipe, although no smoke issued from its top. Presently I saw other discolorations on the landscape, which proved to be the barracks and officers' quarters. The so-called "barracks" were mostly dug-outs, but God be praised! There floating in the storm was Old Glory.
>
> When at last we drove up to my "future home" I found it to be merely another dug-out. I exclaimed, "Why, where is our house?" and before my husband could reply, the sole occupant of the dug-out, who proved to be our "striker," came bustling up the few steps. He apologized and explained that he hadn't started a fire because the Indian[s] had attacked the wood-train the day before, killing two soldiers, and

Lieutenant Frank D. Baldwin and his bride, Alice Black-wood Baldwin, January 1867. Mrs. Baldwin wrote exten-sively of her life at Fort Hark-er, where she lived from Janu-ary to September 1867, giving the only detailed account by a woman of life at the first fort. She and her husband also lived at the new fort, and she provided a comparison of the two.

they were "shy" of wood, but that had he known we were coming he would have managed to gather some odds and ends of wood to keep us warm. The honest fellow was profuse in his apologies, and really was concerned for my comfort and health.

Nobody in the garrison knew of our coming, so we found no prepa-rations for our arrival.

Mrs. Baldwin was clearly distressed upon arrival at her first military station, but she was appalled upon seeing the quarters assigned to the lieutenant to whom she was now attached.

When I first entered my new abode I gazed with disgusted disappointment around the bare, squalid room. Its conveniences were limited to one camp chair, two empty candle boxes and a huge box stove, red with rust and grime, its hearth gone and the space filled with a tobacco-stained hill of ashes, the peak of which was surmounted by "chewed-out quids" of unknown vintage—but they were there! The sordid interior filled me with gloom, scarcely lessened by the four-pane glass window, dirty, dim and curtainless.

Exploring the "inner regions" I found the kitchen scarcely big enough to contain a stove, and such an array of cooking utensils as I had never before beheld lay on the dirt floor and on a packing box, which served duty as a kitchen table! The walls of the kitchen were stayed and supported by logs, while the ceiling was of the same material and covered with dirt. The logs had not been trimmed or cut off, and obliged one to bend low when passing underneath.

The "drawing room," as my soldier-husband facetiously called it, had a board floor, unplaned and full of slivers. Canvas covered the ceiling and dirt sides. It sagged slightly in the center and trembled under the scampering feet of pack-rats and prairie mice. The canvas cover not quite extending on one end, the pack-rats would perch on the beams, rear up on their hind legs, with their bushy tails hanging below, and survey me with their beady eyes. I was an unwonted (and probably unwanted) sight to them, and I am sure they were to me. But finally we became used to each other, although they raced and ran over my head, indifferent to my attempts to oust them with my broom.

My house contained the two rooms—the aforesaid kitchen and "drawing room," one end partitioned off by a portiere of gray army blankets. Behind this barrier was the sole, bedroom accommodations of the dug-out. It was not exactly a "ladies' boudoir." Behind this retreat I cut a small hole in the gray blanket, through which I could peep at anyone who called whenever I sought privacy or had retired for the night.

The deficient accommodations were enough to depress the young bride, and some of her additional experiences were especially demoralizing. Mrs. Baldwin recalled:

The winter of 1867 was exceptionally bitter. The wolves, driven by hunger, were more numerous than usual, and often ventured within the garrison. They howled, fought and yelped, even gnawing and scratching around the kitchen door. Stray scraps and refuse thrown out were devoured as soon as darkness fell and the beasts ventured forth. I was filled with terror at their ominous howling and proximity, and must confess to shedding many a homesick tear.

The next summer the Baldwins moved into new quarters at the second location. Alice recorded that, when the quarters were ready at the new post, "we emerged from our dug-outs and log huts into our respective homes. We soon were settled and felt as if living in palace[s] compared to our former abodes."

Everyone who had lived at the first post undoubtedly shared her elation. In June 1867 orders were issued to tear down the remaining buildings at the first site. The dugouts and some of the old structures apparently remained, however, for they were reported to be occupied by civilian employees and camp followers a year later.

6

Building Fort Harker

The new post, constructed by soldiers and civilian employees, was indeed a notable improvement over the first site. Structures of stones, framed lumber, and logs housed officers, enlisted men, and laundresses, and protected quartermaster, commissary, and ordnance supplies. For the first time Fort Harker had a hospital building (tents had housed the sick and wounded at the old post). The post also offered storehouses, repair shops, sinks (latrines), stables, corrals, and an ice house. Visitors compared the buildings at Fort Harker favorably with those at Fort Riley and other western posts.

But not everyone found the location satisfactory. Colonel Elmer Otis, First U.S. Cavalry and inspector general for the military district, inspected the new post in January 1867 and reported:

> It is situated on the high ground about a mile from the river, where it receives the benefit of all the winds & storms which are prevalent in this country; It is a full mile from the Post to water that is available, & the Post has to be supplied by water waggons hauling it this distance in barrels. The horses also have to go this distance twice a day for water. I can see no reason why the Post should have been put here.

Apparently Otis did not understand the location had been selected to place the post near the railroad, expected to be completed there within a few months. He thought a much better site could be found west of the

Captain Albert Barnitz (1835–1912), Seventh U.S. Cavalry, served briefly at Fort Harker in 1867 and wrote descriptions of the post. His wife, Jennie, was also there for a few days and wrote of her impressions. Captain Barnitz served under Lieutenant Colonel George A. Custer and General Winfield Scott Hancock in 1867. He accompanied Custer to the Battle of the Washita in 1868, where he was injured. He retired from the army in 1870.

first fort, closer to the river and protected by terrain and trees. Nothing came of his recommendation. Construction continued at the new site, although few buildings were completed at the time. Except for two log barracks already occupied at the new site, the rest of the garrison remained at the first location, where quarters were dismal.

In March 1867 Captain Albert Barnitz, Seventh U.S. Cavalry, arrived with his company for duty at the new Fort Harker. Unlike several others who visited the fort during its construction, Barnitz admired the post. He wrote to his wife, Jennie, on March 23, 1867:

> Well, I am much pleased with Fort Harker, in spite of all the disagreeable surroundings. The horses are all in good stables, the men in temporary barracks, and only the officers in tents—which are floored and have board doors &c. The officers' quarters are progressing finely, and they will be indeed handsome—even more pleasant and cozy than those at Fort Riley—and they are beautifully situated.

On March 28 Barnitz described the post's accommodations:

> The men are all in one building—not at all crowded—and the building is well floored, and fitted up with comfortable bunks—each of

Henry M. Stanley, newspaper correspondent, visited Fort Harker in the spring of 1867. He described the post as "a giant wart on the surface of the plain." Stanley later became famous when he found Dr. David Livingstone in Africa in 1871. This 1869 photo is from Stanley's My Early Travels and Adventures in America and Asia *(1895).*

which is provided with a straw mattress, a "bed tick" rather, the building is well lighted (with glass windows) and is heated with three large stoves. We have an abundance of fuel—more than we can use. In rear of the building occupied by the men is another for a mess room, and, at the end of it, a room partitioned off as a kitchen. The mess room has a long table, at which the whole Troop can sit down, and is warmed by two large stoves. In the kitchen is a very large cooking stove. I inspect the barracks and kitchen daily, and see that the cooking is properly done—and indeed the soup, baked beans, roast meat &c. will compare very favorably with the same class of fare provided by many hotels.

It would be interesting to know what the troopers thought of it.

Certainly Henry M. Stanley, reporter for the St. Louis *Missouri Democrat*, viewed the new post much differently in April 1867. He wrote:

Tourists through Kansas would call this place dull enough, but then so much of the interest of a place depends upon its traditions. For a passing traveller, in search of pleasure, it certainly possesses few attractions. . . . When I mention a fort, you need not imagine one of those formidable affairs as built in ancient times, with moat and drawbridge,

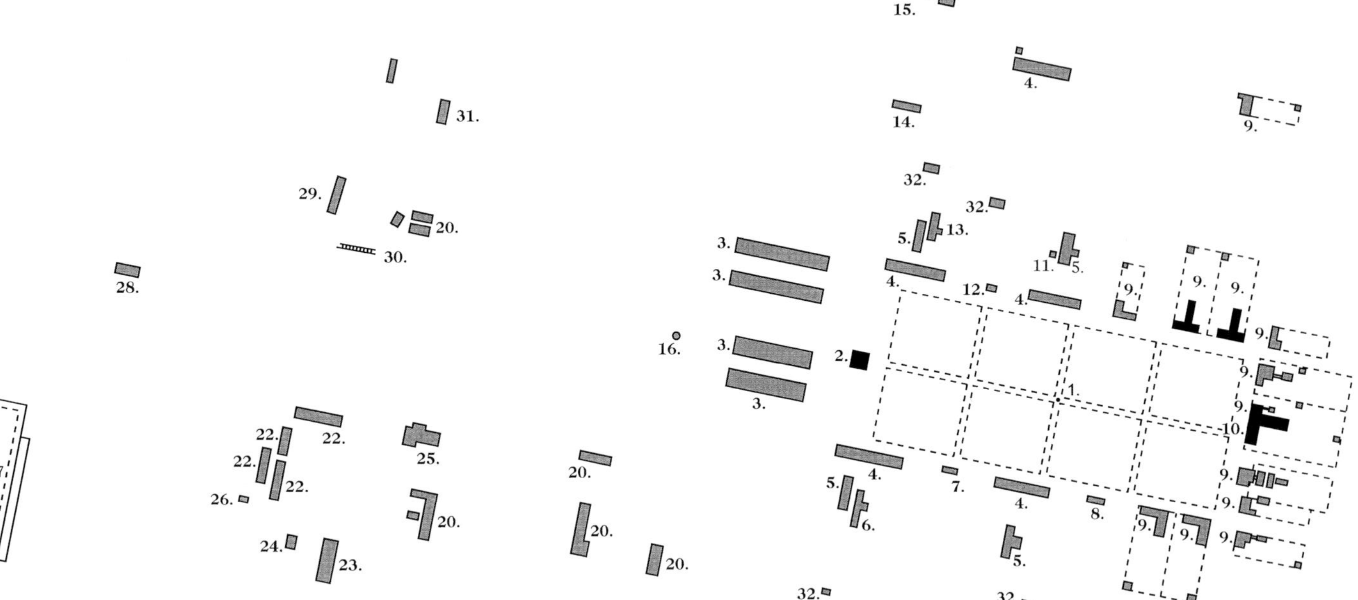

Plan of Fort Harker

towers and battlements, but a simple square, surrounded by some wooden shanties, situated on a gentle eminence, whence there is a commanding view of the great naked prairie. There are neither flowers, shrubs, nor trees planted in its vicinity, and the only vegetation around are the various kinds of grasses. . . . Perhaps the neighborhood of Fort Harker, in summer, when blossoming with flowers, may appear more interesting, but the fort in its present naked state appears like a great wart on the surface of the plain.

William A. Bell, an English physician who joined a railroad survey team on the Plains in the spring of 1867, mentioned the fort briefly in his book *New Tracks in North America* (1870):

> We camped at Fort Harker, thirty-six miles from Salina, a well-built, three-company post, with spacious storehouses filled with the munitions of war, but, like all these military establishments, carrying out in no particular the term "fort."

When completed, the new Fort Harker consisted of many structures arranged around a central parade ground, located near the center of the military reservation of sixteen square miles. The reserve was closed to civilian settlers in order to protect the grass, trees, and water for the army's use. The railroad was permitted to build across the reservation, and a railroad depot was located one-third mile northeast of the garrison.

Four barracks for enlisted men, two of log and two of frame (board and batten) construction, faced each other across the parade ground. One of each type construction stood on the south and the same on the north side, with the log quarters east of the frame buildings. Each barracks housed one company. The dormitories contained double two-tier bunks, with two soldiers up and two below, sleeping head to toe. Post Surgeon Blencowe E. Fryer disliked these beds: "This, as is well known, (aside from any immoral tendency,) is a most objectionable form of bed. All barracks should be constructed so as to give a sufficient area of floor to allow a separate bed to each man placed on it." Fort Harker would be abandoned before the army made that change.

The log barracks conformed to the stockade plan (upright logs with the space between the logs filled with plaster) and included a large dormitory (ninety feet six inches by nineteen feet eight inches) and sergeant's room. The dormitory had five windows on each side. A similar log building behind each barracks, sixty by nineteen feet, contained a kitchen and mess room.

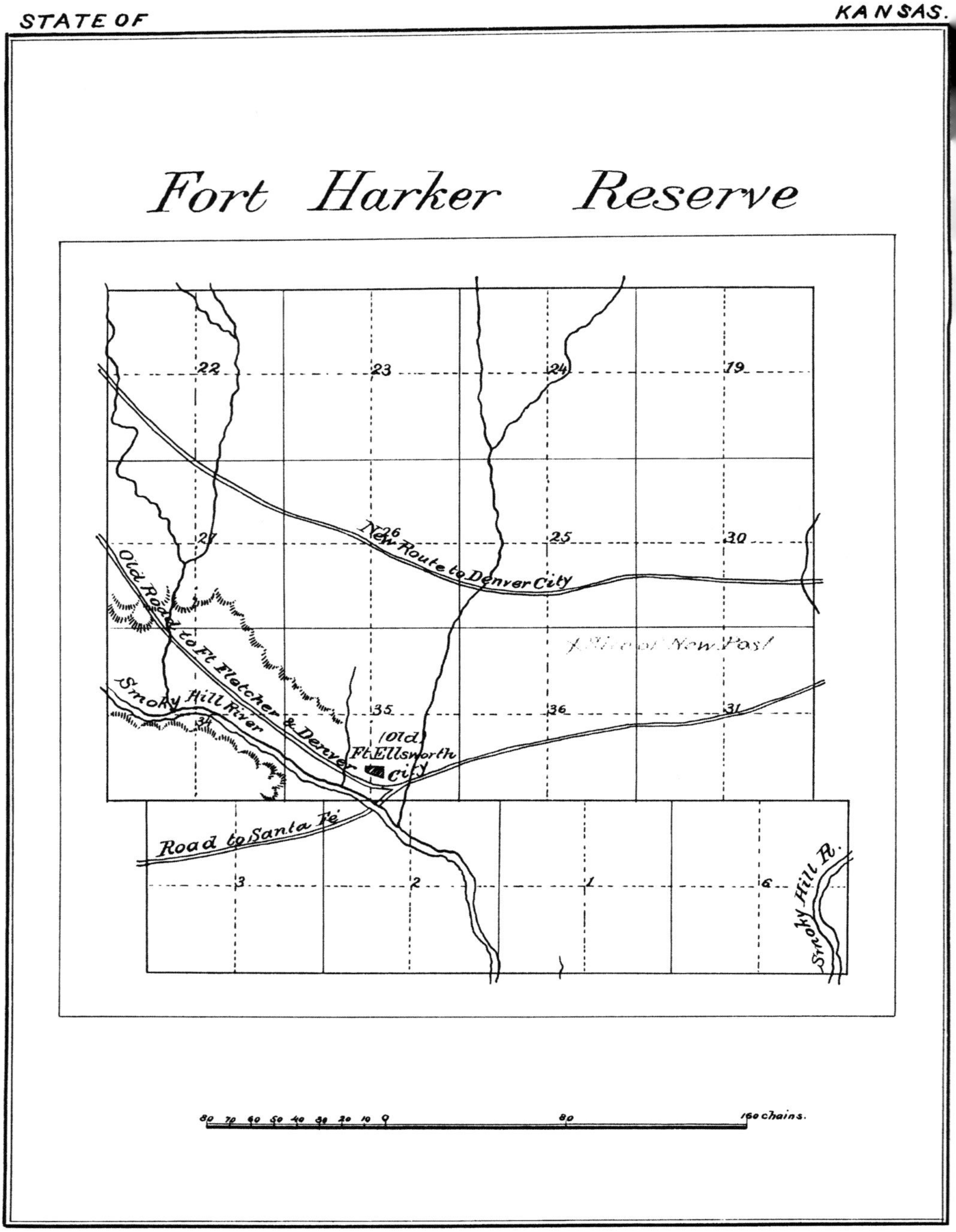

Fort Harker Military Reservation.

Each frame barracks contained two dormitories (each fifty-four feet ten inches by twenty feet eight inches) and sergeant's quarters. Each dormitory had six windows, two on each side and two at the outside end. A building behind each barracks, sixty-five by nineteen feet six inches, contained the kitchen and mess room.

Wood-burning stoves furnished heat. The enlisted men had no separate wash or bathrooms until the spring of 1870 when a bath house was constructed near the springs that supplied water for the post. The sinks or latrines, each a frame building thirteen by eight feet over a pit ten feet deep, stood about 150 yards behind the barracks. A partition through the middle divided the room, with one row of seats containing six holes on each side. The sinks were disinfected daily with lime.

The commanding officer's quarters was one story high, built of sandstone, with nine rooms. There were eight other officers' quarters, two of stone and six of frame construction. Both stone houses and three of the frame quarters were one story, with five rooms. The other three frame officers' quarters were two stories high, with six rooms. Each building had only one kitchen, which was shared when more than one officer (with or without a family) occupied the same structure. All officers' quarters were heated by wood-burning stoves. A privy stood behind each set of quarters.

Eight frame quarters housed laundresses and married soldiers. Each company was permitted four laundresses (the only women the army recognized as having a reason to live at a military post) with their quarters provided and established pay scales set for officers and enlisted men who used their services. Most laundresses were married to enlisted men, but a few were single or married to civilian employees. Surgeon Fryer found the laundresses' quarters inadequate, being small, poorly ventilated, and sparsely furnished, and he declared "none of them are well adapted for the purpose."

Fresh water for the garrison, except for the well at the hospital and wells at three of the officers' quarters, came from two springs three hundred yards west of the post on the banks of Spring Creek, a tributary of the Smoky Hill River. From these springs flowed approximately nine thousand gallons per day, carried through wooden pipes to tanks below. Two or three times each day, water wagons distributed the water to barrels at the barracks and other quarters.

The post had no fire-fighting equipment in 1870, but the post surgeon mentioned a steam-powered pump that had been there earlier had been sent to Fort Riley the previous year. The surgeon noted that "buck-

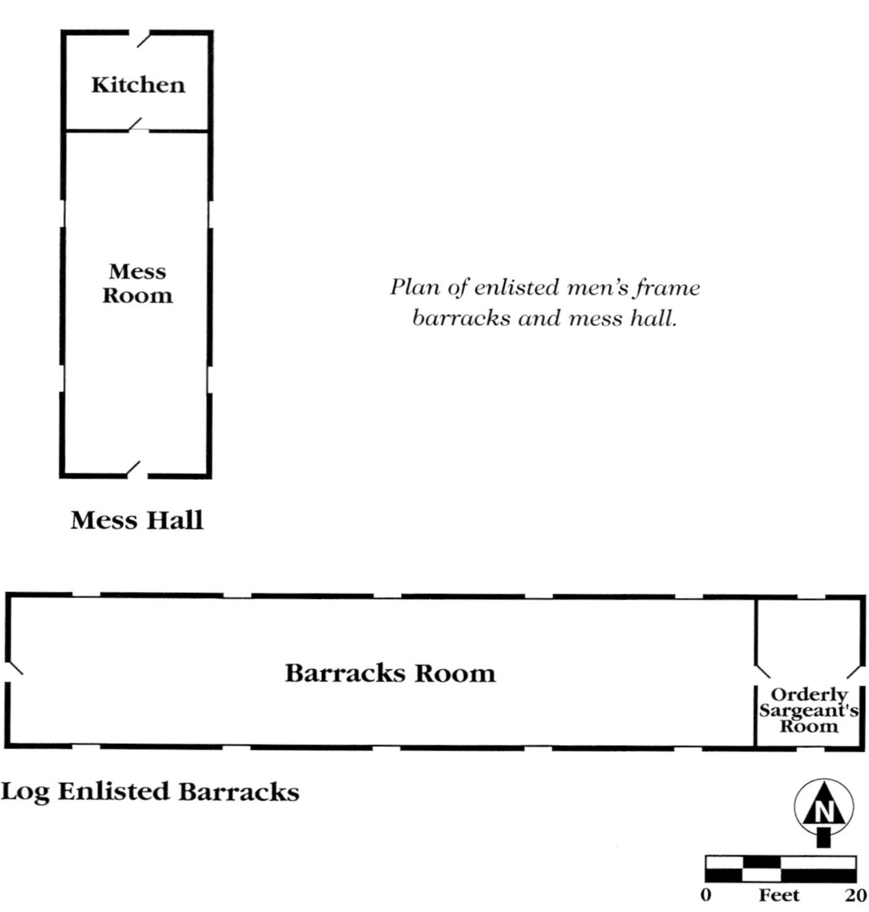

Plan of enlisted men's frame barracks and mess hall.

ets of water are kept in readiness in all the large buildings." This was little help. In September 1868 one of the cavalry stables at Fort Harker was burned completely by a blaze of undetermined origin. The post quartermaster began construction of a new set of stables a few days later.

During the night of November 2, 1869, lightning struck and set fire to the quartermaster corral. Most of the corral burned, along with a row of sheds containing wagons, ambulances, and a medical wagon, all of which were destroyed. Approximately fifty mules died. Fortunately for the rest of the post, the corral was far enough away that the other structures escaped harm.

*Two similar views of Fort Harker with troops assembled on the parade ground.
Photos by Alexander Gardner, 1867, when the post was under construction.*

Three paintings by Hermann Stieffel of Fort Harker in ca. 1871. (Top) looking east; (middle and bottom) looking northeast.

Sanitation and waste disposal were the post surgeon's responsibilities. In 1870 Surgeon Fryer wrote:

> The drainage of the Post is entirely surface though from the elevation is as complete as natural drainage can be. The slops, garbage &c are collected in barrels daily, under the direction of the Police Sergeant (a permanent detail) and hauled a mile from the post and buried. Manure from the stables is hauled the same distance and burned.

Near the railroad tracks north of the post were two large frame storehouses, one for the quartermaster (200 by 50 feet) and one for the commissary (150 by 50 feet). Both were close to a siding so that freight cars could be unloaded directly into them. The commissary department furnished food, and the quartermaster department furnished everything else (transportation, buildings, clothing, shoes, blankets, haversacks, cooking utensils, and camp equipment) except arms and ammunition, which the ordnance department provided. The ordnance storehouse (forty-five by nineteen feet) stood one hundred yards north of the parade ground. From February 1867 to May 1869 Fort Harker was a quartermaster and commissary depot from which supplies were shipped to troops in the field and military posts farther west in Kansas, Colorado, and New Mexico.

The guardhouse, a two-story stone building located west of the parade ground, contained accommodations for the daily guard detail and quarters for inmates. The lower floor housed a guard room (twenty-six by fifteen feet), noncommissioned officers' room (thirteen by eight and one-half feet), and a small storage room. The upper floor, entered from an outside staircase, held prisoners, with two rooms (one seventeen and one-third by twelve feet and the other seventeen and one-half by thirteen feet) and six small cells (each seven by three feet).

The post bakery, located in a frame building (thirty-six by fourteen feet) situated about one hundred yards north of the parade ground, could bake three hundred rations of bread each day. Army surgeons believed fresh bread caused digestive problems, so the loaves remained on the shelf for at least one day before being issued. The post surgeon reported, "As a rule, the bread made is of good quality."

On July 2, 1867, the post bakery temporarily ceased operations. The reason became clear a few days later when the post commander issued the following order: "Owing to the impossibility of getting an enlisted man competent to Bake good and wholesome Bread for this Post, the Post Treasurer is hereby ordered to employ a Citizen Baker at

Fort Harker depot, 1867. Photo by Alexander Gardner.

Commanding officer's quarters.

a Compensation not to exceed $75.00 per month until such time as a Soldier can be found to take his place." The search for "competent" enlisted men continued, and two soldiers were detailed as bakers on August 23, 1867.

A frame ice house, with capacity for four hundred tons, was filled during the winter months with ice cut from the Smoky Hill River. Soldiers from the garrison were assigned to extra duty in the quartermaster department to cut and store the ice, which supplied the garrison and hospital during the summer months.

The post hospital, constructed of sandstone, stood two hundred yards south of the parade ground and faced west. It consisted of a central administration section (one and one-half stories high with a one-story extension to the rear) with two wings (single story) containing the wards on either side. The central portion contained hallways, dispensary, hospital steward's quarters, two offices, and a storage room for medicines. The "T" extension behind contained a mess room, kitchen, and commissary storeroom. The attic was divided into two parts, with a dormitory for hospital attendants on one side and a storeroom for bedding, clothing, and supplies on the other. Each wing was fifty-one by twenty-four feet. A porch (nine feet wide) extended the entire length of the front of the hospital.

Each ward contained twenty beds with iron frames with wooden slats. Surgeon Fryer complained that these were poorly constructed and in constant need of repair. A small table stood beside each bed, and a chair accompanied every other bed. Each ward also had three rocking chairs.

A small room at the south end of the south ward contained bathing and washing equipment. A "good tin portable tub" was available for able patients and all hospital attendants to bathe twice a week. A second tub, kept in the storeroom, could be taken to bedfast patients to provide them a warm bath.

Water for the hospital came from a well located nearby. The hospital had its own garden (three and one-half acres located southwest of the hospital) for vegetables and a cow for milk, cream, and butter. On January 6, 1870, the hospital cow died which, according to the surgeon, "was quite a loss," being the only source for fresh milk products. Rations for patients were furnished by the commissary department, supplemented by purchases at the post sutler's store.

The hospital had no water closets. Patients who were able used the hospital sink, located sixty-eight yards to the rear of the building. A portable pot was available to those who could use it, and bedpans were used by those who were bedfast.

The dead house, a frame building (thirty-four by twelve feet) was located east of the hospital. It was divided into two equal rooms, a dead room and post mortem room. Here the corpses were prepared for burial, which usually occurred within twenty-four hours after death.

Cavalry stables and guardhouse (in background), 1880s.

Guardhouse, post-military occupation.

Junior officers' quarters, post-military occupation.

Remains of the ice house.

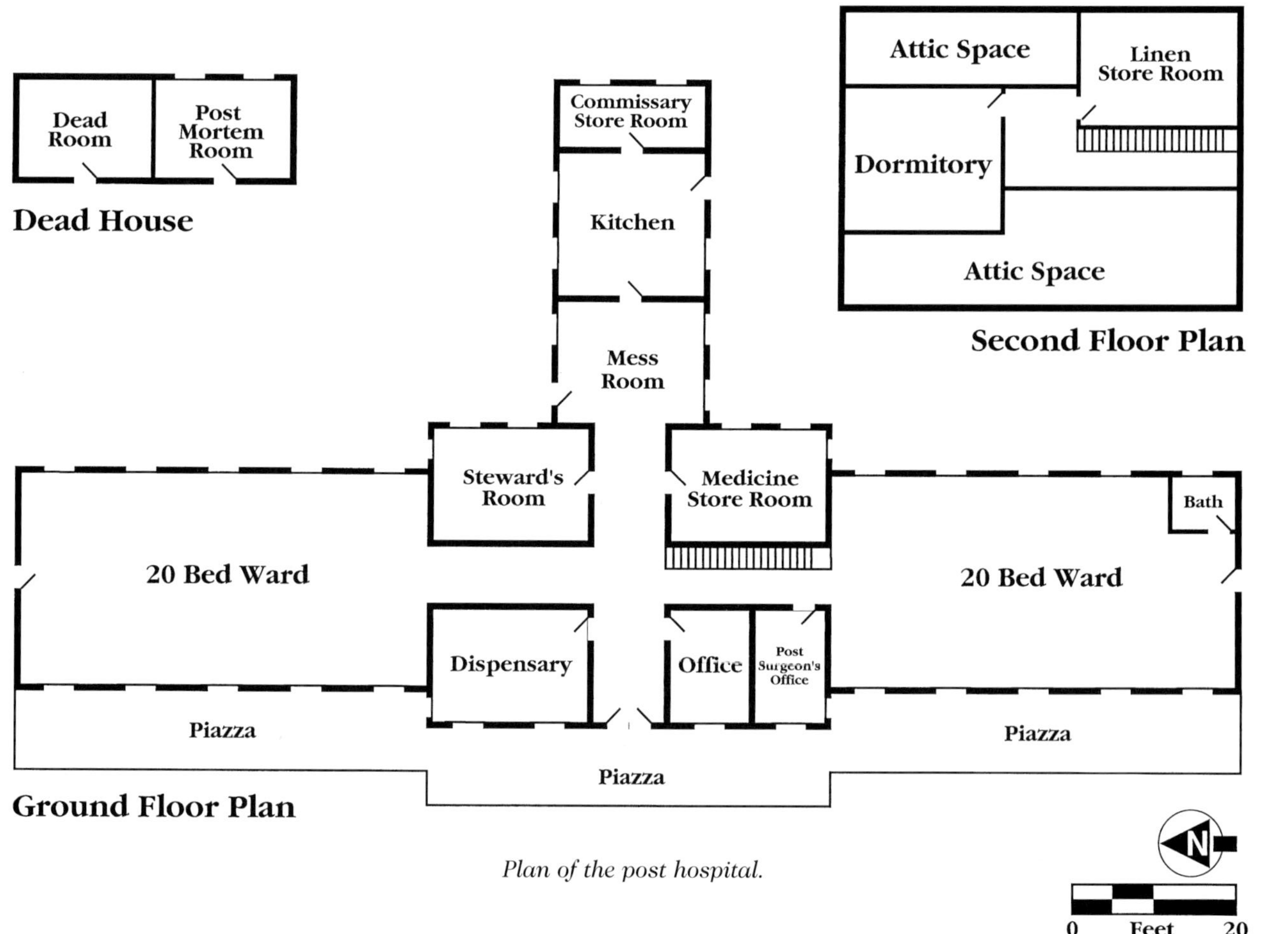

Plan of the post hospital.

The post cemetery (250 by 280 feet) was located one-fourth mile southeast of the post. A six-foot-high fence surrounded it, and trees were planted inside the fence. Records in 1870 show a total of 183 graves, including a number of civilians. Many of those interred could not be identified. When the post was abandoned it had 209 interments, the last (Private Martin DeMan) dated April 3, 1873. In 1898 the remains of about two hundred individuals were removed to the National Cemetery at Fort Leavenworth.

In 1870 the post chapel occupied a portion of the building that had served as the office of the quartermaster depot before the depot closed in 1869. Furniture in the chapel consisted of benches, chairs, and a table. The post chaplain conducted religious services twice each Sunday. One end of the building housed the post quartermaster's office, and the other end, a room ten feet square, served as the post library. The post surgeon described the library as "a light and cheerful room." In 1870 it contained 170 volumes, including histories, biographies, novels, and classics, "with a few practical works." It was open from 9:00 A.M. to 4:00 P.M. daily.

The post contained four frame stables for cavalry horses, each 175 by 39 feet, containing sixty stalls in two rows. Each stable had two rooms, each nine feet square, for forage and storage. The quartermaster corral was located southwest of the post.

Each frontier military post, by direction of the surgeon general, planted a garden to provide fresh vegetables for the garrison. Gardens sometimes failed because of weather and insects. Fort Harker's garden was one-half mile north of the post. A variety of vegetables were grown to supplement the troops' rations. In February 1869, for example, the list of seeds to be purchased for the garden included beans, beets, cabbage, carrots, celery, okra, peppers, potatoes, radishes, cucumbers, corn, lettuce, onions, parsley, peas, turnips, thyme, eggplant, watermelons, nutmeg, and tomatoes. Surgeon Fryer observed in 1870, "Some seasons are too dry for growth, but generally all kinds of vegetables do well."

Other structures at the post included the post surgeon's home, several repair shops, post headquarters office, quarters for the band and chief musician, sergeant major's quarters, and quarters for civilian employees. The post sutler (known as post trader after 1867) was permitted to build a store and quarters on the military reservation. He enjoyed a monopoly for a general store on the post, for which he paid a tax based on the number of soldiers in the garrison. The store offered food, drink, tobacco, clothing, personal items, and recreation at prices set by the

Remains of the hospital.

post council of administration. The sutler at Fort Harker operated a store located north of the post near the railroad tracks. Altogether more than seventy-five structures were constructed at Fort Harker.

Jennie Barnitz spent several days at Fort Harker in June 1867, after visiting her husband in camp with the Seventh Cavalry near Fort Hays and enduring the flood that nearly destroyed that post. She became stranded at Fort Harker for several days because "high water has carried off all the bridges and . . . it will be impossible for us to leave here for a week." She was a guest in the home of the post surgeon and his wife, Dr. George M. and Maria Sternberg, and she described Maria's quarters:

> She is delightfully situated in new quarters—has five spacious rooms—very handsomely furnished, china and silver on her table, excellent servants—then the Doctor has a farm near here, which he has cultivated—& his table is furnished from it—onions, radishes, green peas, etc. etc.

A few days later Mrs. Barnitz left Fort Harker and returned to her home in Cleveland, Ohio. Maria Sternberg died of cholera at Fort Harker on July 15, 1867.

Captain Barnitz returned to Fort Harker in September 1867 and wrote to his wife:

> I find that quite a change has taken place since I left, 6 months ago! The R.R. has come . . . and Ellsworth City has grown up, even since the flood, and innumerable stone buildings are going up at the Post, and broad stone pavement going down, and flashy-looking Artillerymen are standing around in their gay uniforms.

Barnitz visited Fort Harker again in November 1867 and further described the site in a letter to Mrs. Barnitz:

> Really, this is not a very unpleasant place to be stationed now. . . . The Post has changed very much since you were here. . . . All the dwellings are elegantly painted, and grained now. Doors rose-wood color, or something. In the centre of the Parade stands a tall white flag staff, which has cost several hundred dollars, and from its top floats the broad garrison flag, about 20 x 30 feet in size. Around the base of the flag staff is an octagonal, and very handsome fence; the inclosure is entered by an ornamental gate, and ascending a couple of broad steps you find yourself on a platform, or balcony, about 15 or 20 feet in diameter. The boards of the floor radiate from the centre—the flag staff—and are painted brown, or drab. The fence is painted white. At the R.R. track stands a very large new Depot, or ware-house building for storing the quartermaster's supplies. Another large stable has been built, and all are painted white. Two large frame buildings, Captains quarters, containing numerous rooms, are going up on the opposite side of the Parade from what were Dr. Sternberg's quarters while you were here—(and which are now occupied by Genl. [Alfred] Gibbs, who is at present in command of the Post.) The Captains quarters which I have mentioned are two story buildings. There are many other new buildings and out-buildings, which were not here in June. Among others, a very large brown frame building for the Depot Quartermaster's office, and for the occupation of his clerks.

The new Fort Harker definitely was an improvement over the squalid quarters endured by the soldiers at the first post. The fort's enlisted men devoted much of their time to the construction and maintenance of the new post, but the garrison also fulfilled its military duties in the region.

7

Military Duties and Indian Relations, 1864–1866

Although Indians stole most of Fort Ellsworth's horses in August 1864, hostilities decreased along the Santa Fe and Smoky Hill Trails after General James Blunt led an expedition against the bands in September. From Fort Larned his command trailed Indians to a point on Pawnee Fork about seventy-five miles to the west. They overtook a village of Kiowas, Arapahos, and Cheyennes on September 25 and pursued them for several days, killing nine Indians and wounding an undetermined number while losing two soldiers killed and seven wounded. The Indians finally escaped, and Blunt returned his command to Fort Larned. His expedition was credited with reducing hostilities.

A further lull in raiding along the Santa Fe Trail occurred after the Sand Creek Massacre in southeastern Colorado, November 29, 1864. Sand Creek was a clear indication to the Plains Indians that they had no safe havens, a turning point in Indian–white relations. The massacre took place in the autumn of 1864 after peaceful bands of Cheyennes and Arapahos met with government officials near Denver to proclaim their desire for peace. They were sent to camp north of Fort Lyon until peace could be made. There, on Sand Creek, they were attacked by Colonel John M. Chivington and his Third Colorado Cavalry. Although the Indians raised a white flag, men, women, and children were indiscriminate-

51

Photographed here with his staff (unidentified), Major General James G. Blunt (1826–1881), front row center, led troops along the Santa Fe Trail in September 1864 to counter Indian resistance. A native of Maine, Blunt was trained as a physician and practiced medicine in Ohio before moving to Kansas Territory in 1856 to work for the free-state cause. He entered the army as lieutenant colonel of the Third Kansas Volunteers in 1861, was promoted to brigadier general the following year, and achieved success in several battles in Arkansas and Missouri. He became major general in November 1862 and was defeated by William C. Quantrill's guerrillas at Baxter Springs, Kansas, in October 1863. He helped defeat Confederate general Sterling Price in 1864. After the war he lived in Leavenworth and later was confined in a mental institution.

ly slaughtered and mutilated. The Sand Creek Massacre increased tensions throughout the Plains, and the blatant attack was condemned by government officials. For a time, following the attack at Sand Creek, Indian activity decreased along the Santa Fe Trail in Kansas, but Indian resistance increased along the Smoky Hill Trail and western portions of the Santa Fe Trail the following year. The army was held in check, however, while treaty negotiations were again attempted.

Following the end of the Civil War in the spring of 1865, Congress began seeking new peace treaties with the Plains tribes. The treaties of

David A. Butterfield organized the Butterfield Overland Despatch in 1865 to operate over the Smoky Hill Trail between Atchison and Denver, with Fort Ellsworth serving as one of the stage stations. He had been a merchant in Denver and saw advantages to the Smoky Hill route. He did not anticipate Indian problems, however, and soon sold the operation to Ben Holladay.

the Little Arkansas, signed at the site of present Wichita in October 1865, reduced again the incidence of Indian raids along the Santa Fe Trail, with less effect along the Smoky Hill Trail (where raiding continued through late 1865 and into 1866), until the spring of 1867.

During that time important changes in overland transportation also occurred. The Union Pacific Railroad, Eastern Division (UPED), later the Kansas Pacific Railroad, built westward from Kansas City to Topeka and Junction City, where it became the eastern terminus of most stagecoach and freighting operations on the Santa Fe and Smoky Hill Trails. Because rail transportation was faster and cheaper than wagons pulled by draft animals, most commodities were shipped by railroad to the end of the track. Thus the point of embarkation on the overland trails moved westward with the completion of each section of rail lines. The UPED was projected to reach the Fort Harker area in 1867 and, in anticipation of this as previously noted, the post was relocated about one mile northeast of the original site to be near the rail line. Stage and mail services, founded before the railroad was built into Kansas, continued operations from the western terminus of the railroad.

A Cheyenne camp. The Cheyennes, especially the Dog Soldiers, were active in opposition to travelers along the Santa Fe and Smoky Hill Trails.

In September 1865 David A. Butterfield opened the Butterfield Overland Despatch (BOD) over the Smoky Hill Trail from Atchison to Denver. Fort Ellsworth was one of the stage stations on this route, as it also was for the older stage line running between Junction City and Fort Larned. The army soon discovered it could not protect the BOD from Indian resistance.

The Smoky Hill Trail ran through prime buffalo country, and Plains tribes were relentless in their opposition to the trail, stage stations, and travelers on the route. Theodore Davis, reporter and artist for *Harper's Weekly* and *Harper's New Monthly Magazine*, traveled by stagecoach to Denver on the BOD in November 1865. He reported seeing stage stations destroyed and the remains of several employees and travelers "that the Indians had left most barbarously mutilated. These discoveries, following each other so rapidly, caused us to be ever on the alert for an attack."

The attack Davis described came as the coach neared Smoky Hill Station in western Kansas. Davis wrote that, when they were within sight of the stage station, "we glanced back to see the country over which we had passed, and discovered, within sixty yards of the coach, a band of

Theodore Davis, reporter and artist, portrayed an Indian attack on a stage-coach in his drawing Here They Come, published in Harper's New Monthly Magazine, *July 1867.*

nearly a hundred mounted Indians, charging directly toward us." The coach reached the station where the Indians besieged the passengers and employees until the next day, when soldiers arrived and dispersed them. Davis reported that within a short time Indians had killed eight BOD employees, stolen nearly two hundred mules, and killed several soldiers. His coach arrived safely in Denver on December 2, 1865. To keep this road open, however, additional military support was essential west of Fort Ellsworth.

The army established several new forts in 1865 to protect both the Smoky Hill and Santa Fe roads. These included Forts Fletcher (later Hays) and Wallace on the Smoky Hill route in western Kansas, and Camp Nichols in present Oklahoma and Forts Aubrey and Dodge in southwest Kansas on the Santa Fe Trail. Soldiers at all these locations also helped protect the survey and construction parties of railroads building westward across the Kansas Plains. Troops from these posts could escort wagon trains and stagecoaches, and in small parties they could protect stage stations and, later, railroad stations. These new posts were all supplied from the quartermaster depot at Fort Ellsworth.

At first, however, the additional posts were unable to prevent hostilities along the Smoky Hill route. Because of losses suffered from Indian

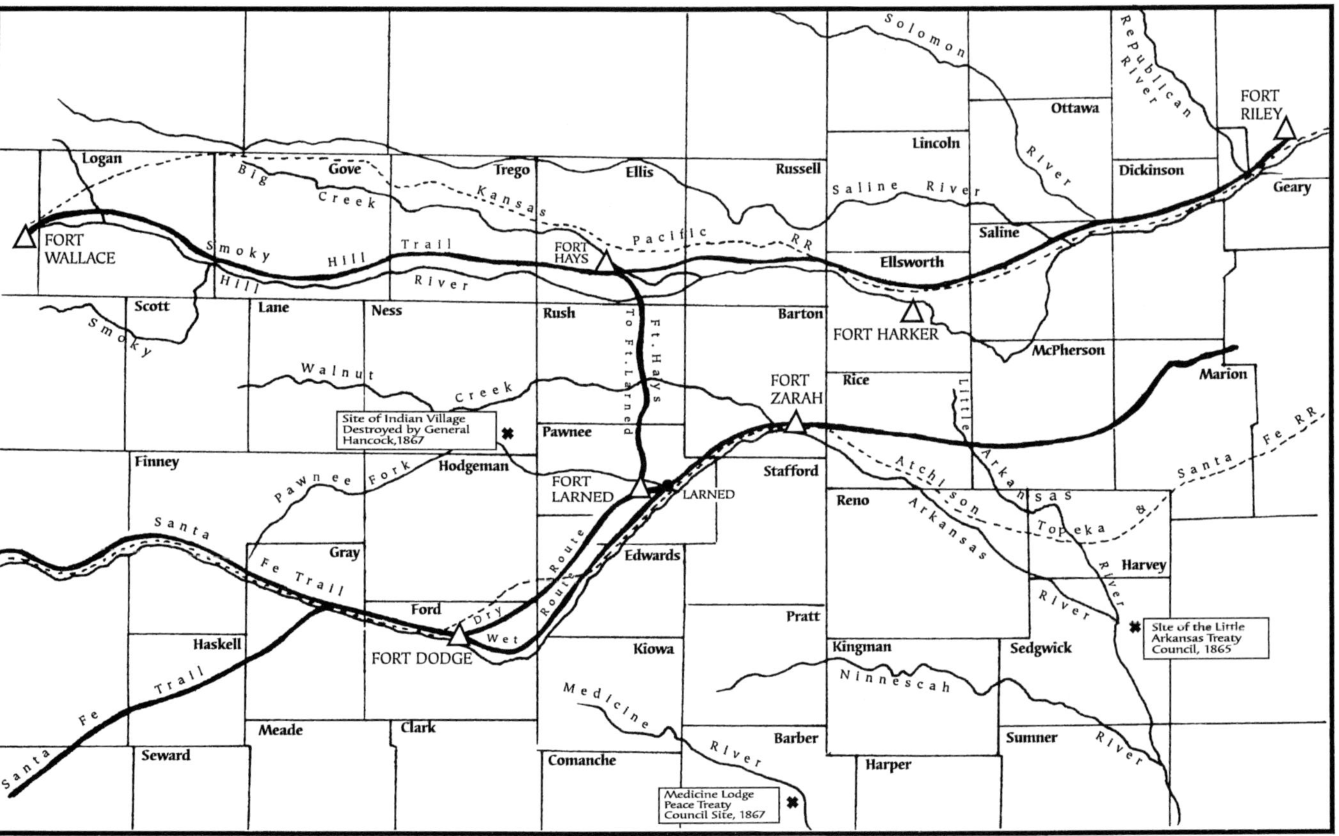

Kansas trails and railroad lines in relation to military posts, from Fort Riley to the state's western border.

raids, Butterfield sold the BOD to Ben Holladay in March 1866. Holladay, facing continued Indian resistance, sold the line to Wells Fargo and Company a few months later. Wells Fargo decided the risks were too great and sold the operation to the United States Express Company in February 1867. With improved military protection, this company kept the stage line open between the end of the railroad track and Denver until the railroad reached Denver on September 1, 1870.

But the peace that followed an increased military presence and the treaties of the Little Arkansas in 1865, did not last. Some defiant leaders of Cheyenne, Arapaho, Kiowa, and Comanche tribes had not signed the treaties and would not abide by them. They refused to stay on reservations and returned to the area of Kansas north of the Arkansas River to hunt buffalo and collect their promised annuities at Forts Larned and Dodge.

In May 1866 Captain John Green reported that Indians had burned one of the stage stations on the Smoky Hill Trail. The superintendent of the stage line requested military protection from Fort Ellsworth, including guards for some stations and an escort with each coach as it traveled between Fort Ellsworth and Fort Fletcher. The military quickly complied.

Simultaneously, efforts were made to negotiate with the Indians and urge them to keep the treaties. Edward W. Wynkoop, who had served as an officer in the volunteer army during the Civil War, was appointed special agent to meet and confer with those who had not signed the treaties. He held several meetings with members of the Cheyenne, Arapaho, Kiowa, and Comanche tribes during 1866, including one at Fort Ellsworth in August of that year, to persuade them to accept the terms of the treaties. They did not do so.

Wynkoop held council with eight principal chiefs of the Cheyenne (including Black Kettle) and Arapaho tribes at Fort Ellsworth on August 11, 1866. He delivered to them some of the commodities that had been promised the previous year. The special agent reported the Indians were happy to see him and said they feared the government had forgotten them and would not fulfill the terms of the treaties. These chiefs promised to keep the agreements, but they wanted everything that had been promised to them, including reparations for the Sand Creek Massacre (six hundred horses and replacement of equipment), return of two children captured at Sand Creek, and annuities. Wynkoop assured them he would deliver everything pledged to the tribes as quickly as possible.

The chiefs apologized for raids perpetrated by young warriors along the Smoky Hill Trail, explaining that some of their people were not

Edward Wanshear Wynkoop (1836–1891), left, posing with "Texas Jack" Crawford, served as sheriff in western Kansas Territory (present Denver, Colorado) before the Civil War and was an officer in the First Colorado Infantry during the war. He commanded Fort Lyon, Colorado Territory, prior to the Sand Creek Massacre in November 1864 and later investigated that affair. Wynkoop commanded the escort for the commissioners at the Little Arkansas treaty negotiations in 1865, and he resigned from service the following year to become agent for the Cheyenne, Arapaho, and Plains Apache tribes. His agency was briefly at Fort Ellsworth before it moved to Fort Zarah and then Fort Larned. He opposed General Winfield Scott Hancock's treatment of the Indians in 1867 and protested the burning of the village on Pawnee Fork. Likewise, he disapproved of the winter campaign, fearing it would punish peaceful Indians, and he resigned as agent at the time of the Battle of the Washita in 1868.

ready to give up the Smoky Hill country, and others believed the government was not keeping the treaties. Wynkoop believed the Indians were somewhat justified in violating the 1865 treaties. The terms of the treaties, especially the surrender of all rights to the Smoky Hill country, had not been fully explained. More important, however, was the government's failure to deliver promptly the promised annuities, which led those Indians who had, as well as those who had not, signed the treaties to conclude that the United States was not keeping its end of the bargain.

The potential for renewed hostilities also increased with the flow of liquor to soldiers and Indians. In May 1866 Captain John Green, Second Cavalry, commanding Fort Ellsworth, complained that unscrupulous traders were selling whiskey to the Indians. He feared the consequences, noting that "unless the sale of Liquor in the Indian Country can be prevented there is great danger of another outbreak." Wynkoop reported that Indian Agent I. C. Taylor, of Fort Zarah, was "constantly in a state of intoxication" and that Taylor was supplying liquor to the Indians who were "frequently drunk." Soldiers from Fort Ellsworth who had visited Fort Zarah on escort duties returned in a state of intoxication.

Wynkoop requested immediate action to shut down the flow of alcohol. Nothing was done, however, and the following month Captain John Page, Third U.S. Infantry, commanding Fort Ellsworth, sought help from Kansas governor Samuel J. Crawford:

> I would respectfully bring to the notice of your Excellency the Whiskey Ranches between Saline, this Post, and Posts beyond this in the State of Kansas. My Soldiers are continually drunk, these Ranchmen, selling and giving them liquor on credit. As I interpret the Law this is Indian Country, and it is my duty to destroy all spirituous liquor brought into it.

> I would respectfully ask your Excellency to inform me if these Ranchmen have authority to sell liquor with a License beyond Saline. I consider it Indian Country. It will be, as has been, the chief cause of Indian troubles. These Ranchmen are as a general class unprincipled men and I am confident that through their means the Indians receive quantities of liquor.

> Trains passing through the teamsters become intoxicated. Indians visit their camps and naturally some insult is offered.

> I have written to your Excellency as I wish to fully understand the laws of the State upon this subject.

> The evil is increasing every day. Citizens and officers of the Army report that between this Post and around Zarah, they see the Indians continually under the influence of liquor.

The governor's response has not been found, but the illicit liquor traffic continued, and the tense environment of Indian–white relations was further aggravated by alcohol abuse on both sides. Rational thought and action, essential to a peaceful settlement, was less likely when liquor emboldened aggressive responses. At various times Indians, Indian agents, and soldiers were reported as intoxicated.

When reports of Indian raids were received in the late summer of 1866, troops from Fort Ellsworth were dispatched to protect settlers. On September 1, 1866, two lieutenants and seventy-six cavalrymen from Fort Ellsworth were ordered to proceed "to the vicinity of the Forks of the Solomon River, Kansas, and thoroughly scout the country reported

Black Kettle was a leading peace chief of the Southern Cheyennes. He signed treaties and urged accord with Euro-Americans, believing his people would be destroyed in a war with the U. S. Army. His village at Sand Creek, Colorado Territory, was attacked by Colonel John M. Chivington in November 1864. Black Kettle survived and supported the treaties of the Little Arkansas, 1865, and Medicine Lodge, 1867. He was at Fort Ellsworth for a conference in 1866. He and his wife, along with many members of his band, died at the Battle of the Washita in November 1868. His life and death exemplified the tragedy of the Plains Indian wars.

to have been recently the scene of Indian depredations." According to the post commander, "It took every pistol, carbine and saddle at this Post to arm and equip this detachment, so that the portions of the Cavalry Companies remaining are entirely without arms and horse equipment." He doubted the post could defend itself if attacked, and he requested reinforcements and equipment.

While troops from the post were in the field, Wynkoop received appointment as regular agent for the Cheyennes, Arapahos, and Plains Apaches. He established his agency at Fort Ellsworth in October. In mid-October, before Wynkoop assumed his new duties, a council began at Fort Zarah between Special Indian Agent W. R. Irwin and leaders of the Cheyenne and Arapaho tribes. Some of their annuities were available. Unfortunately for negotiations, reparations from the Sand Creek Massacre (the two Indian children and the promised horses) were not available to present to the Indians.

Agent Irwin asked the chiefs to agree to amendments to the Little Arkansas treaties, which changed the location of permanent reservations

William Bent (1809–1869) operated Bent's Old Fort on the Arkansas River near present La Junta, Colorado, 1833–1849. In 1853 he built Bent's New Fort, which was sold to the government in 1859 to become part of Fort Wise (later Fort Lyon), Colorado. Bent served as Indian agent in 1859 and advocated the construction of additional military posts, such as Fort Harker, to help control the Indians. He married Owl Woman, a Cheyenne, and after her death married her sister, Yellow Woman. Some of his half-Cheyenne children chose to live in the Indian tradition. His sons Charles and George were known to raid with other Cheyenne warriors.

(the reserves would be entirely in present Oklahoma rather than a portion in Kansas south of the Arkansas River). If they refused, plans were to withhold annuities and store them at Fort Ellsworth until the chiefs accepted the changes. There was concern that the Cheyenne Dog Soldiers would pledge to remain peaceful until the annuities were delivered, after which they would resume raiding.

The conference at Fort Zarah failed, and no agreement was reached. The Cheyennes wanted the two children from Sand Creek returned, but the children had not been located. They wanted the horses, but these had not yet been purchased. All tribes, including the Kiowas and Comanches (some of whom had joined the conference), wanted guns, ammunition, and powder promised them but not delivered. William Bent, present at this meeting, had a supply train on the road with these items, and he agreed to sell them to the Indian Bureau.

The Dog Soldiers, who had not been present at the Little Arkansas negotiations, now objected to the terms of that treaty and compelled the Cheyenne peace chiefs who had signed the treaty to refuse to accept the amendments. The Dog Soldiers were unwilling to vacate the Smoky Hill region and opposed the construction of the railroad along that route.

Ignoring their very real concerns, Agent Irwin declared that some factions of Cheyennes were "not disposed to be peaceful" because of their excessive drinking.

Irwin stated that the abundance of whiskey, supplied by unscrupulous traders, rendered a solution to disagreements impossible. Fortified with alcohol, the mood of some Indian leaders was threatening. Adding to the animosity was Charles Bent, half-Cheyenne son of William Bent, whom Irwin claimed did "much to cause discontent and is a bad man" and was considered one of the sources of whiskey. William Bent urged Irwin to arrest his son, who was often intoxicated, but Irwin considered that unwise because Charles was "very popular and had great influence among the Indians." When Charles threatened to kill his father, William Bent left the council, embarrassed by his son and realizing that no agreement was possible. He sold the supplies in his wagon train before leaving. Arms were distributed to the Kiowas and Comanches but withheld from the Cheyennes and Arapahos.

During the conference word was received that some Dog Soldiers led by Bull Bear had burned a stage station in western Kansas and killed two employees. The council ended without any agreement. Agent Wynkoop offered to distribute annuities to the Cheyennes, Arapahos, and Plains Apaches at Fort Ellsworth, where he arrived and commenced his new duties on October 26, 1866. For the time being, the fort was the agency for these tribes.

Wynkoop called the Cheyenne and Arapaho peace leaders to another conference at Fort Ellsworth, believing they would sign the amendments to the Little Arkansas treaties if the Dog Soldiers were not there to influence them. The Indians did not come to the fort and demanded arms and ammunition promised to them. Wynkoop realized no agreement was possible without first fulfilling the promises made to the tribes. He moved the agency temporarily to Fort Zarah in an attempt to revive negotiations. The Indians agreed to meet near that post for delivery of annuities.

Another delay resulted, however, when a Cheyenne man killed a New Mexican herder, employed by William Bent, on November 9, 1866, near Fort Zarah. Despite this, the Arapaho leaders eventually signed the amendments, and their annuities were brought from Fort Ellsworth and distributed. Negotiations with the Cheyennes broke down when they refused to surrender their man who, while intoxicated, had killed the herder, but the chiefs condemned that outrage. They also signed the amendments, and their annuities were brought

Bull Bear, a chief of the Cheyenne Dog Soldiers, provided leadership in the resistance to the Euro-American invasion of the buffalo range and lands of the Plains tribes. In 1866 he urged the peace chiefs not to accept amendments to the Little Arkansas treaty, and he raided along the Smoky Hill Trail in protest against the treaty. In 1867 he asked General Winfield Scott Hancock not to move troops to the Cheyenne and Sioux village on Pawnee Fork, the same village Hancock burned a few days later. Bull Bear was engaged in the subsequent warfare along the Smoky Hill Trail and in the attack on Forsyth's Scouts at Beecher Island in September 1868. He joined his people on the reservation in present Oklahoma in 1869 but never fully accepted reservation life.

from Fort Ellsworth for distribution. Annuities for the Plains Apaches also were delivered, and all tribes received arms and ammunition. The peace factions of these tribes accepted the agreements, but the recalcitrant factions, especially the Cheyenne Dog Soldiers, were not included and were expected to resume hostilities the following spring. Wynkoop moved his agency to Fort Larned on November 26, stating it was a more central location than Ellsworth or Zarah to serve the tribes.

In anticipation of additional raids, more troops were stationed along the Smoky Hill Trail. On November 12 troops marched from Fort Ellsworth to protect stage stations at Lost Creek (approximately twenty-eight miles west) and Fossil Creek Station (approximately forty-three miles west). A sergeant and twenty privates occupied each place, with rations for one month. They built stockades to live in and protect the stage stations, equipment, livestock, and employees. In addition to an ample supply of ammunition, each detachment carried "tents, axes, spades, shovels, nails, and such carpenters tools in small amount as may be necessary." The detachments were relieved each month by other troops from the post.

In December, Wynkoop reported that Indians in his agency were "quiet and peaceable," noting he had never known them to be "more peaceably disposed." He warned, however, that "many false rumors in regard to Indian Affairs in this section of the Country are circulated but they are usually originated by parties to whom it would be a matter of personal interest to inaugurate an Indian war." Wynkoop did not identify who those people might be, but his prediction proved to be true.

Those who supplied the army, carried freight to the frontier posts, and transported supplies and equipment into the field for military expeditions could reap fortunes if fighting continued. The railroads wanted the Indian threats removed, but some politicians and merchants, according to General William T. Sherman, were "resolved on trouble for the sake of the profit from military occupation."

Newspaper reporters, including Milton W. Reynolds of the Lawrence *State Journal*, later accused Kansas governor Samuel J. Crawford and other officials of promulgating the fear of a general Indian uprising so they could raise a regiment of Kansas militia for federal service. Henry M. Stanley, correspondent for the St. Louis *Missouri Democrat*, and S. F. Hall, reporter for the *Chicago Tribune*, expressed this position: Hall wrote, "Governor Crawford does not breathe all peace but favors hostilities which will require enlistment of 10,000 Kansas troops." Crawford later was charged with accepting a bribe from one of the railroads. An investigation exonerated him, but he did receive 640 acres of land from the railroad company. Thus rumors of war may have had as much to do with politics and economics as with the disposition of the Plains tribes.

While rumors spread of an Indian uprising in 1867 and Indian agents pursued negotiations with various tribal factions, the soldiers at Fort Ellsworth, now Fort Harker, continued to guard stage stations along the Smoky Hill Trail and the Fort Riley–Fort Larned Road. They also provided escorts for stagecoaches and wagon trains when military commanders deemed these necessary for safe passage. Primarily, however, the garrison at Fort Harker was busy at the new post, constructing buildings, performing fatigue and guard duties, and doing everything necessary to maintain the post and keep it clean. In addition to these duties, they were called upon for extensive field operations in 1867.

8

The Zenith Year, 1867

For Harker experienced its most significant and active year during 1867. In that year the garrison moved to a new post, which the soldiers with the help of civilian employees constructed; the District of the Upper Arkansas, headed by Colonel Andrew J. Smith, Seventh Cavalry, moved its headquarters to Harker; the Hancock Expedition (which is explained later) stopped at the post and was supplied from its storehouses, and supplies also were shipped from there to posts farther west; the railroad reached the fort and nearby town of Ellsworth in July; a cholera epidemic took a heavy toll during the summer; and escort duties occupied a good portion of the garrison during much of the year. By the following year the railroad and much military activity had moved farther west, and Fort Harker entered its declining years.

During the winter of 1866–1867, as previously noted, rumors abounded that Plains tribes were preparing a major assault on the overland trails in the spring of 1867. To counter this anticipated renewal of Plains warfare, Major General Winfield Scott Hancock, commanding the Department of the Missouri, was determined to march a large military force onto the Plains to intimidate the tribesmen and force them, by military action if necessary, to the reservations, where they had agreed to go under the terms of the Little Arkansas treaties. As previously mentioned, Fort Harker became the base of supplies for the Hancock Expedition.

The expedition left Fort Riley in March 1867 and marched to Fort Harker, where two troops of Seventh Cavalry in the post garrison were added to the assemblage. In preparation for this campaign, on March 28, 1867, Captain Alfred Gibbs, Seventh Cavalry, commanding Fort Harker, issued orders enumerating how these cavalrymen from the post were to be equipped and packed for field duty, providing a rare (only such detailed description known to exist) and informative depiction of those details:

I. In order to carry out the provisions of Extract IV G.O. No. 39, C.S. from Dist. Hd. Qtrs. the Commanding Officers of F & G Troops 7th U.S. Cavalry will hold themselves and their Companies in readiness to march in an hours notice. To this end the Companies will be fully Armed and equipped for the field. Horses will be sharp shod, and old shoes now on (serviceable) will be taken off and re-set. Saddle equipment will be carefully examined and deficient parts replaced or repaired. Sabres will be ground on the edge 2/3 of the way down from the point and up to the reinforce on the back. One suit of undercloth-ing, one blouse, and one extra pair of boots will be allowed to each man, hats will be left behind. Spare clothing will be carried in a blanket on the Cantle of the Saddle, poncho on top of blanket. Overcoat, properly rolled up on pommel of Saddle. Each man will be furnished with one days cooked rations. Extra shoes and nails in right pouch of each Sad-

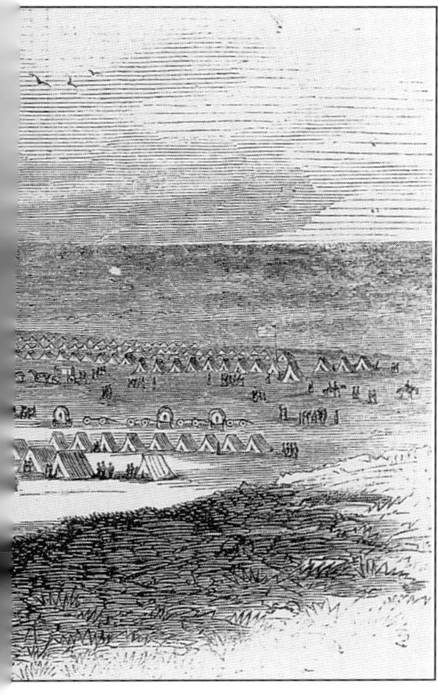

This Theodore Davis sketch of the Hancock Expedition at Fort Harker appeared in Harper's Weekly, *April 27, 1867.*

dle. Knapsacks and spare baggage of each Company will be marked with the owners name and Company, boxed up and turned in to the Qr. Mr. Dept. for Safe Keeping.

II. Any unserviceable Horses will be invoiced to the Dept. Qr. Master at Fort Riley and turned over to the Post Qr. Master for transportation.

III. The Company Wagons will carry five days subsistence for the Officers and Enlisted Men, their Camp and Garrison Equipage, five days short forage for the teams, and twenty boxes of Ammunition.

IV. One Wall Tent and one Common (A) tent will be drawn for the Company Officers of each Company.

V. All surplus Ordnance and Ordnance Stores will be turned over to Bvt. Col. V. K. Hart Capt 37th U.S. Infantry who will receipt for same.

The Hancock Expedition, after remaining at Fort Harker for two days, marched on to Forts Zarah and Larned. After an expected conference with Cheyenne leaders at Fort Larned did not occur, in part because of a spring blizzard that dumped several inches of snow, Hancock marched his fourteen hundred troops up Pawnee Fork some thirty-two miles to a large village of Cheyennes, mostly Dog Soldiers, and Sioux.

Those Indians, fearing an attack such as had occurred at Sand Creek in 1864, fled their village. Hancock's troops took possession of the three

General Winfield Scott Hancock (1824–1886), renowned for his Civil War record, commanded the Department of the Missouri in 1867. Anticipating a major Indian uprising on the Plains, Hancock led a strong force from Fort Riley via Fort Harker to Fort Larned and beyond. His capture and burning of the Cheyenne and Sioux village on Pawnee Fork in April 1867 resulted in increased hostilities known as "Hancock's War." He was replaced the following year by General Philip H. Sheridan. Hancock ran for president in 1880 and was defeated by James A. Garfield.

Major Alfred Gibbs, Seventh U.S. Cavalry, commanded Fort Harker during portions of 1867 and 1868. He was an important officer in the newly organized Seventh U.S. Cavalry, for he was a strict disciplinarian and created the famous regimental band. A graduate from West Point in 1846, he served in the Mexican War, Indian campaigns, and the Civil War. He was wounded by an Apache lance in 1857 and remained in poor health. Unable to continue in the field with his regiment in 1868, he died at Fort Leavenworth on December 25 of that year. His position with the regiment was filled by Marcus A. Reno.

Colonel Andrew J. Smith, Seventh U.S. Cavalry, led the regiment from its organization in 1866 until 1869. He was at Fort Harker as commander of the District of the Upper Arkansas. He never took command of the Seventh Cavalry in the field, leaving that to Lieutenant Colonel George A. Custer. Smith retired in 1869 and was succeeded as colonel by Samuel D. Sturgis.

hundred tipis and contents, most of which they later burned. This unprovoked action touched off an Indian uprising on the Plains, fulfilling the predictions of the previous winter. Troops at Fort Harker, as well as every other post on the Plains, saw increased activity.

On June 17, 1867, forty Indians attacked six settlers on Plum Creek, eighteen miles southwest of Fort Harker, and chased them nearly eight miles as the settlers fled to the protection of the post. The settlers lost five horses to the attackers, but they thought they may have wounded eight Indians during the running fight. This band also attacked Plum Creek Station and captured eight horses and seven mules. The same day a wagon train headed for Fort Dodge was attacked; one man was killed and another wounded. This train had "slipped past Fort Harker without getting an escort." Possibly the post had too few troops to provide an escort because only thirty-eight men were available for duty in the garrison. Due to Indian raids, some of the railroad construction crew abandoned their work. As soon as they were available, however, troops were sent to protect the workers.

During 1867 troops from Fort Harker provided escort and special guard duties 195 times (a record for any military post in the post-Civil War era), primarily accompanying supply trains and stagecoaches. The quartermaster depot, under the direction of Captain Henry Inman,

sent supplies to troops in the field and to other military posts (*see* Appendix), and it employed more than two hundred civilians during much of the year. In September 1867 the following transportation animals and equipment were inventoried at the quartermaster depot: 162 horses, 1,586 mules, 337 army wagons, 7 two-horse wagons, and 31 ambulances. An unknown number of these were away from the post at the time delivering supplies.

In July 1867, as additional troops were needed to garrison Kansas forts, the Eighteenth Kansas Cavalry (comprising four companies) mustered into the service and was outfitted at Fort Harker. The Eighteenth Kansas, which had been raised by Governor Crawford to assist federal troops, was led by Major Horace L. Moore and served on the Plains until late October 1867, when the volunteers mustered out of service at Fort Harker.

Also during the summer of 1867 epidemic cholera struck Fort Harker and other Kansas forts. At Harker alone nearly fifty soldiers died, and more than fifty civilians succumbed, including Maria Sternberg, wife of post surgeon George M. Sternberg. Alice Baldwin recalled that "few escaped its ravages. Persons were smitten without warning, and so virulent was the disease that the living were unable to bury the dead." Some deaths were more tragic than others. Mrs. Baldwin noted, "among the

During the late spring and early summer of 1867 black soldiers of the Thirty-eighth U.S. Infantry were stationed at Fort Harker to assist with protection of stage stations, railroad construction crews, and travelers on the Smoky Hill and Santa Fe Trails. This artist's rendition of black troops attacking Indians near Wilson Creek Station, approximately twenty-five miles west of Fort Harker, appeared in Harper's Weekly, September 7, 1867.

victims were a sergeant and wife who left four little children, alone and homeless."

Captain George A. Armes, Tenth Cavalry, was in camp near Fort Harker with a company of his regiment. His younger brother, William Edward (Eddie) Armes, scheduled to begin school at West Point in the autumn, was visiting the captain for a taste of military life. On July 3 Captain Armes left Eddie in camp while he led a scouting expedition. The following day Armes recorded in his diary:

> I returned this evening from my scout, and after making my report to Gen. A. J. Smith, he broke to me the sad news of the death of my brother, whom I had left yesterday morning in camp in the best of spirits and apparently in excellent health. He was taken with cholera, and died before three o'clock that afternoon. It was the saddest news I could receive.

In addition, seven troopers in Armes's company died of cholera within ten days.

The disease spread along the trails to other military posts, killing soldiers, quartermaster department employees, and other civilians. Although cholera often was fatal, many of its victims survived. Fort Harker surgeon Sternberg, with the help of surgeon John Williams Brewer,

Henry Inman (1837–1899) enlisted in the army in 1857 and later was commissioned an officer. He was assigned to the quartermaster department during the Civil War and served as post and district quartermaster at Fort Harker. He directed supply operations for the Hancock Expedition of 1867 and the winter campaign of 1868–1869. He was dismissed from service in 1872 because of chronic discrepancies in his accounts. He later entered journalism, worked for various Kansas newspapers, and wrote several books (some of questionable veracity).

George A. Armes was at Fort Ellsworth/Harker several times during his brief military career in Kansas. He first served as a lieutenant in the Second U.S. Cavalry and later as captain in the Tenth U.S. Cavalry. His younger brother died of cholera in camp near Fort Harker in 1867. Armes was engaged in several Indian battles in 1867–1868. He was frequently in trouble and, by his own count, was court-martialed nine times. He later wrote an account of his military career, Ups and Downs of an Army Officer *(1900)*

George M. Sternberg was post surgeon at Fort Harker during the cholera epidemic of 1867. After losing his wife to the disease, he went to Fort Riley in the fall of that year where he remained, with the exception of a few months, as post surgeon until 1870. In 1893 Sternberg was promoted to surgeon general of the army. In 1867 his father and brothers had moved to a farm near Fort Harker, from which they became world-famous fossil collectors. The family is memorialized at the Sternberg Museum of Natural History in Hays, Kansas.

Surgeon John W. Brewer came to Fort Harker during the cholera epidemic of 1867 to assist Dr. Sternberg, who was exhausted from battling the disease and distraught from the death of his wife.

tried to fight the spread of the disease by isolating victims and employing strict sanitation, including boiling the drinking water. They did not know it at the time, but the disease is primarily spread through contaminated water. Sternberg's efforts in fighting cholera, and the reports he later wrote about dealing with the epidemic at Fort Harker, helped earn him promotions that culminated with his appointment as surgeon general of the army in 1893. The disease ran its course at Fort Harker within two months but had disrupted military action against the Indians during that time.

In October 1867 another series of peace negotiations were conducted with several Plains tribes at Medicine Lodge Creek. The Indian Commission and the supply trains for the conference were escorted from Fort Harker. The treaties of Medicine Lodge were signed the same month by many of the Cheyenne, Arapaho, Kiowa, Plains Apache, and Comanche tribal leaders. They agreed to remove to reservations in present Oklahoma in return for additional annuities and other promises.

These treaties also failed. Some Indians, especially the Cheyenne Dog Soldiers, refused to accept the terms and resolved to continue fighting. The U.S. Senate did not approve the treaties until the following summer, and appropriations to provide the promised annuities did not pass until August 1868. By that time the Indians concluded the U.S. government had no plan to keep the treaties and had returned to the region north of the Arkansas to collect annuities and hunt buffalo. The war of 1868 was the consequence.

9

The Final Years, 1868–1873

After waiting for and not receiving the promised annuities in the spring of 1868, some tribesmen began to harass passing wagon trains, begging for food and other items. In June a party of Cheyennes raided the Kansa Indians on their reservation near Council Grove, avenging the death of several Cheyennes. Troops came from Forts Harker and Riley to protect the Council Grove area, and additional troops were stationed along the overland routes of travel.

Alcohol was still a problem in 1868 for both Indians and soldiers, which may have increased the possibility of conflict. Lieutenant Howard B. Cushing, Third Infantry, encamped with his company near Fort Harker in May 1868, complained to district headquarters about liquor among his troops:

> I have the honor to state that about a mile below my camp, on the opposite side of the river, there is a Ranch in which bad whiskey is kept for sale, and many of the men of my command are from time to time under the influence of liquor, and knowing that they have no money wherewith to purchase it—not having been paid since their enlistment, averaging from 3 to 4 months—they must obtain the whiskey in exchange for articles of government clothing &c issue to, or stolen by them.

It was especially feared that Indians inclined to be peaceful might become belligerent under the influence of alcohol. Reportedly, some

General Philip Henry Sheridan (1831–1888) was a career officer who achieved fame as a cavalry commander during the Civil War. He replaced General Winfield Scott Hancock as commander of the Department of the Missouri in February 1868. He developed plans to defeat the Plains Indians, which included forming Forsyth's Scouts (partially organized at Fort Harker) and devising the winter campaign (partially planned at Fort Harker before Sheridan moved his headquarters to Fort Hays). In 1869 Sheridan became commander of the Military Division of the Missouri, and in 1883 he was promoted to general-in-chief of the army. He was at Fort Harker several times.

early raids in 1868 were by young men who had been drinking and dared each other to commit acts of violence. Liquor was not the cause of Indian grievances—after all, they were fighting to preserve a way of life—but the possible effects of alcohol on Indian–white relations in 1867 and 1868 should not be dismissed.

In preparation for warfare, a military post was established on June 11, 1868, near present Wichita. Originally called Camp Davidson, the name was changed in November 1868 to honor Lieutenant Frederick Beecher, killed at the Battle of Beecher Island in September of that year. Camp Beecher was occupied until October 1869. Throughout its existence, the post was supplied from and under the command of Fort Harker.

As feared, Indian hostilities did begin during the summer of 1868. When they learned their annuities still were not available in July 1868, some Cheyennes raided settlements along the Saline, Solomon, and Republican Rivers (reports of eyewitnesses supported claims that some of the men were fortified with whiskey). Kansas governor Crawford appealed for more federal protection. General Philip H. Sheridan, who had replaced Hancock as department commander, directed that three military stations be established among those settlements. These stations, located on Spillman Creek and the Saline River, were placed under the jurisdiction of Fort Harker's commanding officer, who sent men and supplies to garrison them and under whose direction they served.

In 1868 De B. Randolph Keim, reporter for the *New York Herald*, accompanied General Sheridan and his troops in the field. His subsequent book *Sheridan's Troopers on the Borders* (1870) describes activities at Fort Harker and the outbreak of the Indian war:

> Intelligence of the conduct of the Indians on the Saline and Solomon was conveyed, by fugitive settlers, to Fort Harker. The garrison was at once put in condition for active service. As a hasty means of relief to the settlements, Lieutenant Colonel [Frederick] Benteen, was ordered out with one company of the 7th cavalry. On August fourteenth, he arrived at Spillman's creek, while the Indians were attacking. His unexpected appearance so alarmed the savages that they took to flight, thus sparing the lives of the settlers at that point.

General Sheridan, at department headquarters at Fort Leavenworth, was immediately apprised of the situation. He moved his headquarters and staff to Fort Harker for a brief time before moving on to Fort Hays. While at Harker, according to Keim, Sheridan determined that "His only course was a resort to force." Keim continued:

> On the twenty-fourth of August, he accordingly issued a general order which served as a declaration of war. By the middle of September, the Indians in hostile numbers had made their appearance in all parts of the Department west of Fort Riley, north as far as the Platte river, to the Arkansas in the south, and westward into Colorado. The lines of travel demanding protection were the Kansas Pacific railway, for a distance of over two hundred miles, the stage routes, and lines of travel from the terminus of the railroad to Denver, nearly two hundred miles, and into New Mexico, over four hundred miles. Besides these the settlements on the Saline, the Solomon, the Republican, and the Smoky Hill, needed some means of defence, while the posts of Forts Riley, Harker, Hays, and Wallace, along the railroad, Forts Lyon and Bascom in the west, Forts Dodge, Larned, and Zarah on the Arkansas, with an outpost at the mouth of the Little Arkansas, and Forts Arbuckle and Gibson, in the Indian Territory, required suitable garrisons. . . .
>
> With this insignificant force, available for field duty, that is eight hundred cavalry, active hostilities were commenced.

Captain Frederick W. Benteen (1834–1898) led Troop H of the Seventh Cavalry from 1866 to 1882. He commanded Fort Harker during part of 1868 and established an outpost at Spillman Creek in August of that year. He was with George A. Custer at the Washita and the Little Big Horn battles.

The troops stationed at Spillman Creek (approximately four miles northwest of present Denmark, Kansas), erected a blockhouse and corral. This outpost was occupied until 1870, and troops there were relieved by replacements from Fort Harker each month.

During the summer of 1868 Indian hostilities increased along the overland routes and railroad. General Sheridan raised a special force of Indian scouts, under command of Major George A. Forsyth, to pursue those suspected of conducting raids, and Sheridan began planning for a campaign against the Indians' winter encampments in present Oklahoma. Because the soldiers in the field seldom could locate Indians, who seemed to disappear into the landscape as they divided into smaller and smaller units, leaving no trails to follow, Sheridan hoped a unit of civilian scouts, trained in tracking, might be able to pursue and punish these bands. More important, however, was Sheridan's conclusion that the best time to find and attack Plains Indians was when they were encamped for the winter, unable to escape without difficulty. Reinforcements came when Samuel Crawford resigned as Kansas governor and took leadership of the Nineteenth Kansas Cavalry.

Forsyth's Scouts, as the unit of fifty volunteers led by two army officers was known, were raised at Forts Harker and Hays. They proceeded to Fort Wallace in September 1868; from there they pursued Indians who had attacked a wagon train near Sheridan, Kansas, about fifteen miles east of the post. These scouts were attacked by a force of Cheyennes and Sioux on the Arickaree Fork of the Republican River in eastern Colorado Territory on September 17, 1868, and were besieged there for several days. Forsyth was severely wounded, and his subordinate officer, Lieutenant Frederick Beecher, was killed (giving his name to the location of the Battle of Beecher Island and to Camp Beecher). Surgeon John H. Mooers and several scouts also were killed, and many more were wounded. They were rescued after suffering for nine days. Sheridan abandoned the thought that civilian scouts might be able to deal with the mobile Plains Indians where the military seemed unable to find and engage them.

His other plan, however, was more successful. The winter campaign, organized at Fort Hays, and outfitted in part from Fort Harker but mostly from Fort Dodge, achieved its goal following the Battle of the Washita, November 27, 1868, in which Black Kettle and many of his fellow Cheyennes were killed, fifty-three were captured, and some eight hundred ponies were destroyed. Except for the more belligerent of the Plains tribes, such as the Cheyenne Dog Soldiers, the Indians who had signed the treaties of the Little Arkansas and Medicine Lodge moved to the reservations. Those who continued resistance in Kansas were defeated the following year.

In the spring of 1869 a band of Cheyenne Dog Soldiers, led by Chief Tall Bull, raided among settlements in north-central Kansas. They were pursued and defeated at the Battle of Summit Springs in Colorado Territory in July 1869. That marked the end of resistance from the Dog Soldiers, most of whom remained on the reservation thereafter.

Troops from Fort Harker continued to guard stage stations, railroad stations, and military camps along the Saline and Solomon Rivers through 1871. The next few years witnessed occasional outbreaks when small bands escaped from the reservations and during the Red River War (1874–1875), but none of these were general uprisings, and damages and deaths were limited to small areas and numbers. The so-called last Indian raid in Kansas, the escape of the Northern Cheyennes from the reservation in present Oklahoma, occurred in 1878.

Long before that, in the early 1870s, Fort Harker had fulfilled its missions when most Indian resistance in Kansas had been eliminated and Harker was far removed from any scenes of hostilities. Railroad progress

Samuel Johnson Crawford (1835–1913) came to Kansas Territory in 1859 as a young attorney. During the Civil War he served as captain of the Second Kansas Cavalry and colonel of the Eighty-third U. S. Colored Infantry. He resigned from service in 1864 when he was elected governor of Kansas, and he was reelected in 1866. In 1867 he authorized the Eighteenth Kansas Cavalry, organized at Fort Harker, to fight Indians in northwest Kansas. He resigned as governor on November 4, 1868, to assume command of the Nineteenth Kansas Cavalry, which participated in the winter campaign of 1868–1869.

Major George A. Forsyth, Ninth U.S. Cavalry, was chosen by General Sheridan to organize and command a company of fifty scouts, known as Forsyth's Scouts, in the summer of 1868. These scouts were recruited at Forts Harker and Hays, sent to Fort Wallace to find and punish resistant Indians, and were defeated at Beecher Island in September of that year. Forsyth was severely wounded during that battle and nearly died. He recovered and served in the army until his retirement in 1890. He wrote two books, both published in 1900: The Story of the Soldier *and* Thrilling Days of Army Life. *He died in 1915.*

rendered the post's quartermaster depot obsolete. The Union Pacific, Eastern Division, became the Kansas Pacific in 1869 and reached Denver in 1870. The Atchison, Topeka and Santa Fe reached Fort Dodge and Dodge City in 1872. Military supplies could be shipped by rail far beyond Fort Harker. The fort, no longer needed, was abandoned in 1872 and reoccupied briefly a few months later before it closed forever in 1873.

During the ninety-two months of occupation for which records are available, the Fort Harker garrison averaged 242 officers and men. The number of troops fluctuated widely, however, from a low of 45 in August 1865 to a high of 614 in June 1867. The two years of most active military operations, 1867 and 1868, saw the highest monthly averages of troop strength: 411 in 1867 and 297 in 1868.

The foundation of the garrison comprised the infantry, often supplemented by one or more companies of cavalry. A battery of artillery was stationed at the post briefly in 1867. Various volunteer units composed the garrison until December 1865, when regular army companies arrived. Troops of the Second, Sixth, and Seventh Cavalry regiments served at Fort Harker periodically from 1865 to 1873. One company of black troops from the Tenth Cavalry was stationed at the post for two months in 1867 during the cholera epidemic. Soldiers from the Third, Fifth, Thirteenth, Nineteenth, and Thirty-seventh regiments of infantry were represented sometime during 1865–1872. Black troops from the Thirty-eighth Infantry headquartered at Harker from May 1867 to April 1869, the period of most intense military action and escort duty. They also suffered losses to cholera.

Civilians and military personnel lived on the military reservation. In March 1869 Colonel N. S. Davis, inspector general for the department, reported that, in addition to military structures at Fort Harker, there were

> scattered about in an irregular manner, and covering quite an extensive area, some eighty-five (85) to ninety (90) structures, being board shanties, log huts, dugouts, wood & canvass erections &c. of a variety of shapes and dimensions, occupied by Gov't employes & others, which in my opinion should be removed or demolished, many are dirty and even filthy, in one of which the first case of cholera at Fort Harker occurred as is reported, many are believed to sinks of iniquity and corruption and from their character location and use are a pest to the Post and service.

In May 1869 the commanding officer reported that some fifty families, with a population of about 150, resided in dugouts, tents, and "miserable hovels" near the post. The post commander noted, "Many of these

Nelson A. Miles (1839–1925) compiled a fine record during the Civil War and was awarded the Congressional Medal of Honor for gallantry during the Battle of Chancellorsville, May 2–4, 1863. He was a colonel in the Fifth U.S. Infantry when he commanded Fort Harker during portions of 1869, 1870, and 1871. He later played a major role in several Indian campaigns. He rose to the rank of general and was general-in-chief of the army from 1895 until his retirement in 1903. Of the twenty-six commanders of Fort Harker, he was the only colonel and held the best-known overall military record.

people have no visible means of support, they are not only a nuisance, but the uncleanly conditions of their quarters will endanger the health of the garrison during the coming warm season." He requested authority to remove them from the reserve. It was not determined how many were removed, and civilians still resided near the post the following year.

The only federal census taken during the life of Fort Harker was in June 1870 when Colonel Nelson A. Miles, Fifth Infantry, was commanding the post. The post returns for that month showed a garrison strength of 203 soldiers, with 43 civilian employees. A number of the troops counted in the post return were away from the post on detached duty when the census was taken. The census records show a large number of civilians in relation to military personnel. The census taker counted 129 officers and enlisted men, enumerated as 14 officers, 17 noncommissioned officers, 21 musicians, 70 privates, and 7 in the guardhouse. A listing of 164 civilians included 8 officers' wives and 9 children, 7 noncommissioned officers' wives and 6 children, 5 private soldiers' wives and 9 children, 38 male government employees and 4 wives and 12 children, 21 male railroad employees and other male civilians and 6 wives and 8 children, and 15 single women several of whom had 16 children. Single women had various duties including laundress, seamstress, maid, cook, servant, nurse, hospital matron, and one woman visiting her sister who was wife of the post surgeon. Of the 293 persons enumerated, 122 had been born outside the United States. Of the 129 military personnel counted, only 58 were natives of the United States. Clearly the army depended heavily upon immigrants to fill the ranks. There was an imbalance of the sexes, as one would expect at a military post, with 218 males and 75 females. The average age was twenty-four, with the oldest individual being forty-eight and with twenty children under the age of six.

The food rations at the post were, according to the post surgeon in 1870, "both ample and sufficiently varied." Basic daily rations, set by military regulations, included, per man: meat (12 ounces of salt pork or bacon, or 20 ounces beef (fresh, salted, or canned); 18 ounces flour or fresh bread, or 12 ounces hard bread (hardtack, which soldiers referred to as "cast iron biscuits"), or 16 ounces corn meal; 2.4 ounces beans or peas or 1.6 ounces hominy or rice; 1.6 ounces coffee or .32 ounces tea; 2.4 ounces sugar, and small amounts of salt, pepper, and vinegar. Each soldier also received a ration of soap and candles. The post garden provided fresh vegetables in season.

Additional food could be purchased at the post commissary (*see* Appendix), the post trader's store, or from area farmers. Ellsworth County had approximately five hundred farmers in 1870, according to the post surgeon, who declared they "are hard working industrious people." Items and prices for produce available from local farmers in 1870 were milk (40 cents per gallon), eggs (25 to 40 cents per dozen), chickens (50 to 75 cents each), potatoes (50 to 80 cents per bushel), turnips (40 to 60 cents per bushel), and cabbages (10 to 30 cents per head). Other items in season included onions, melons, and berries.

The *Military Hand Book & Soldier's Manual of Information*, a small pocket-size book issued to each soldier, included suggestions and recipes for food preparation. When in garrison, the rations were cooked in quantities in the company kitchen and served in the mess room. In the field, soldiers cooked their own rations, or pooled their rations and cooked them together in small groups. Most soldiers complained about the food's quantity and quality.

THREE OF FORT HARKER'S COMMANDING OFFICERS.

Major Joel Elliott,
Seventh U.S. Cavalry.

Captain Simon Snyder,
Fifth U.S. Cavalry.

Captain Adna R. Chaffee,
Sixth U.S. Cavalry.

THE COOK'S CREED

Cleanliness is next to godliness, both in persons and kettles. Be ever industrious, then, in scouring your pots. Much elbow-grease, a few ashes, and a little water, are capital aids to the careful cook. Better wear out your pans with scouring than your stomachs with purging; and it is less dangerous to work your elbows than your comrade's bowels. Dirt and grease betray the poor cook, and destroy the poor soldier, while health, content, and good cheer should ever reward him who does his duty and keeps his kettles clean. In military life punctuality is not only a duty, but a necessity, and the cook should always endeavor to be exact in time. Be sparing with sugar and salt, as a deficiency can be better remedied than an overplus.

Remember that beans, badly boiled, kill more than bullets; and fat is more fatal than powder. In cooking, more than in anything else in this world, always make haste slowly. One hour too much is vastly better than five minutes too little, with rare exceptions. A big fire scorches your soup, burns your face, and crisps your temper. Skim, simmer, and scour, are the true secrets of good cooking.

Source: Captain James M. Sanderson (Commissary of Subsistence), *Camp Fires and Camp Cook; or, Culinary Hints for the Soldier* (Washington, D.C.: Government Printing Office, 1862), 4.

By the early 1870s Fort Harker was obsolete. The railroad had rendered the quartermaster depot unnecessary, and it had been closed in 1869. The scene of action had moved far from the post. The two log barracks were badly deteriorated by the summer of 1871, when a board examined "and reported them to be in an unsafe condition and of course not fit for occupancy—that the walls had spread, that a large majority of the logs were thoroughly rotten, and that the weight of the roof (which is cottonwood logs) which weight is increased much during rains, may bring these buildings down at any time." They were vacant at the time. Some repairs were made to these buildings in October 1871, when they apparently were occupied again.

In 1871 General John Pope, commander of the Department of the Missouri, recommended that Fort Harker be abandoned. Despite a plea from the Kansas legislature to keep it an active post, the order to abandon Fort Harker was issued April 2, 1872. Most of the garrison had already departed, leaving a commissioned officer, surgeon, noncommissioned officer, and five privates in charge of the post to guard the buildings and prevent looting. This detachment left in October, and the post was reoccupied temporarily during the winter of 1872–1873 by some of the Sixth Cavalry. The last troops left in April 1873.

10

After Fort Harker

The buildings and the military reservation were left in charge of a noncommissioned officer. The land and buildings could not be sold until the War Department transferred the property to the Department of the Interior. In 1875 the quartermaster department hired a civilian to look after the former military post.

In April 1875, at the request of the Smithsonian Institution, a building at the post was assigned to paleontologist Charles H. Sternberg, brother of George M. Sternberg (former post surgeon at Fort Harker), who needed space for the fossils he was collecting. It is not known how long this arrangement lasted.

In late 1875 the buildings at the old post were evaluated to see what could be salvaged and utilized at other forts, particularly Fort Hays and Fort Lyon. Nothing more was done. In 1876 the Kansas legislature requested that the post be turned over to the state for educational purposes. No action was taken. In August 1876, at the request of the Kansas Pacific Railroad, General William T. Sherman, commanding general of the army, granted permission to house temporarily seven hundred emigrants from Russia at Fort Harker.

In 1878 the secretary of war notified Congress that the Fort Harker military reservation was no longer needed for military purposes and requested that it be transferred to the Department of the Interior. Squatters resided on the reservation in 1878, anticipating that the land would soon be open for settlement. During 1878 the remains of military per-

Charles H. Sternberg, brother of Surgeon George Sternberg, moved with the Sternberg family to a farm near Fort Harker in 1867. Locating numerous fossils in the area, he and his sons eventually became world-famous collectors. The family's work is honored at the Sternberg Museum of Natural History in Hays, Kansas.

sonnel and their families interred in the Fort Harker cemetery were removed to the national cemetery at Fort Leavenworth. Not until 1880, however, did Congress act, authorizing the transfer of the military reservation and buildings to the Department of the Interior to be sold to the public.

The military reservation was opened for individual settlers under U.S. land laws. The land containing the buildings was sold to a speculator who again sold the property to an Ohio firm, Henry Johnson and Company, for the establishment of a town. Apparently little happened, although a post office was established there in 1881. In 1885 the old fort was sold to another Ohio syndicate. The following year the town of Kanopolis was established, with the old fort as its base. On March 30, 1886, the Kanopolis post office was established, and great plans for this community ensued. Located near the center of Kansas, the founders believed it would be an ideal location for the state government offices. Accordingly an area was set aside for a future state house and other government buildings. The town was laid out to accommodate 150,000 res-

The former guardhouse of Fort Harker today serves as the Fort Harker Museum in Kanopolis, operated by the Ellsworth County Historical Society.

The commanding officer's quarters at Fort Harker, obviously modified, now serves as a private residence in the town of Kanopolis.

One of two remaining junior officers' quarters. Recently acquired by the Ellsworth County Historical Society, the organization plans to rehabilitate the building into a museum.

The porch fronts of the two junior officers' quarters. The quarters in the background is a private residence.

idents. So far neither the state government nor the 150,000 citizens have moved to Kanopolis, which today has a population of 600.

Today four of the original stone buildings from the fort are in use in Kanopolis. The former guardhouse serves as the Fort Harker Museum, operated by the Ellsworth County Historical Society, and three former officers' quarters are residences. These are small reminders of what was once a large military complex and for a brief time, in 1867, one of the busiest military posts on the frontier. No great battles are associated with Fort Harker, and no major incidents occurred there. It performed its missions well, including supply depot, command headquarters, and active military post. It served the needs of the state and the nation during an era of rapid transition from frontier to settled land. Fort Harker is one of eight military posts of the Kansas Forts Network, and its history is a part of the frontier military heritage.

Commanding Officers of Fort Harker

An officer is listed for every month in which he served any time as commanding officer. The post was named Fort Ellsworth from September 1864 to November 1866.

Second Lieutenant Allen Ellsworth, Seventh Iowa Cavalry,
    August–September 1864

Lieutenant Henry W. Garfield, Seventh Iowa Cavalry,
    September1864–February 1865

Captain Curtis Clark, Seventh Iowa Cavalry, February–October 1865

Major Hiram Hilliard, Seventeenth Illinois Cavalry,
    October–November 1865

Lieutenant Charles H. Lester, Second U.S. Volunteers,
    November–December 1865

Lieutenant Ferdinand Edwin de Courcy, Thirteenth U.S.Volunteers,
    December 1865

Captain John Green, Second U.S. Cavalry, December 1865–May 1866

Captain Kilburn Knox, Thirteenth U.S. Infantry, March 1866

Lieutenant Colonel Innis N. Palmer, Second U.S. Cavalry,
    May 1866–September 1866

Captain John H. Page, Third U.S. Infantry, September–October 1866

Captain Dangerfield Parker, Third U.S. Infantry,
    October 1866–January 1867

Major Alfred Gibbs, Seventh U.S. Cavalry, January–April,
September–November 1867, October–December 1868

Captain Verling K. Hart, Thirty-seventh U.S. Infantry, April–July 1867

Captain John N. Craig, Thirty-eighth U.S. Infantry, July–October 1867,
September-October 1868

Captain C. C. Parsons, Fourth U.S. Artillery, August–September 1867

Major Joel Elliott, Seventh U.S. Cavalry, November 1867–April 1868

Captain D. H. Brotherton, Fifth U.S. Infantry, January, April–May
1868, April–May, August 1869, October–November 1870,
April–June 1871

Captain Frederick W. Benteen, Seventh U.S. Cavalry,
May–September 1868

Captain E. H. Lieb, Fifth U.S. Cavalry, December 1868–April 1869

Colonel Nelson A. Miles, Fifth U.S. Infantry, May 1869–October 1870,
January–April 1871

Major J. G. Tilford, Seventh U.S. Cavalry,
November 1870–February 1871

Captain Simon Snyder, Fifth U.S. Infantry, June–October 1871

Major C. E. Compton, Sixth U.S. Cavalry, October 1871–May 1872

Lieutenant E. L. Randall, Fifth U.S. Infantry, May–October 1872

Second Lieutenant Henry P. Kingsbury, Sixth U.S. Cavalry,
December 1872–January 1873

Captain Adna R. Chaffee, Sixth U.S. Cavalry, January–March 1873

FORT HARKER MONTHLY AGGREGATE GARRISON

The post was named Fort Ellsworth from September 1864 to November 1866.

YEAR	JAN	FEB	MAR	APR	MAY	JUN	JUL	AUG	SEP	OCT	NOV	DEC
1864								NA	NA	82	82	82
1865	172	181	179	177	189	189	NA	45	230	412	63	114
1866	114	108	105	63	297	391	387	381	134	368	363	373
1867	372	351	324	325	491	614	468	312	394	538	371	372
1868	391	399	365	350	348	349	345	345	336	114	113	112
1869	110	111	112	66	65	115	119	154	180	180	239	311
1870	308	308	182	179	174	203	178	177	177	450	436	433
1871	425	424	259	156	154	67	67	67	65	117	222	223
1872	217	217	223	79	3	3	3	2	2	0	0	78
1873	159	161	161									

The aggregate of officers and men includes those sick in the hospital, confined in the guardhouse, assigned to extra duty, and temporarily away from the post on escort or guard duty. Thus the actual number of enlisted men available for routine duty at the post was only a portion of the aggregate total.

The following list of employees in the quartermaster department at Fort Harker was recorded during an inspection of the post on March 2, 1869. The quartermaster depot was closed later that spring, and many of these civilian employees were discharged.

Position	No.	Position	No.
Storekeeper	1	Painters	2
Clerks	11	Tinner	1
Quartermaster Agent	1	Cooper	1
General Superintendent	1	Sailmaker	1
Engineer	1	Watchmen	1
Forage Master	1	Foreman of Laborers	1
Veterinary Surgeon	1	Laborers	96
Corral Master	1	Cooks	5
Packers	6	Depot Wagonmaster	1
Messengers	2	Assistant Depot Wagonmaster	1
Carpenters	10	Wagonmasters	2
Blacksmiths	8	Assistant Wagonmasters	4
Assistant Blacksmiths	4	Master of Transportation	1
Saddlers	5	Teamsters	82
Wheelwrights	5	Scouts & Guides	2
Plasterer	1	Ostlers	15
		TOTAL	287

TOTAL MONTHLY PAYROLL $12,351.50

Officers and enlisted men could purchase additional supplies from the commissary storehouse. Prices were set by adding cost and, if shipped in, transportation. Sizes and weights in the following chart were not given, but some products probably sold by the pound, some by the can, some by the gallon, and some a single item. Note that many prices are quoted in fractions of a cent.

Item	Price	Item	Price
Pork	.14	Family Flour	.0521
Bacon	.1645	Assorted Crackers	.18
Shoulder	.104	Java Coffee	.335
Fresh Beef	.099	Choice Tea	.65
Flour	.031	Ct. Loaf Sugar	.155
Hard Bread	.0375	Crushed Sugar	.17
Corn Meal	.0238	Granulated Sugar	.1425
Beans	.06	Syrup	1.43
Peas	.04	Molasses	.82
Rice	.10	Lime Juice	2.00
Hominy	.0275	Citric Acid	1.00
Rio Coffee, Green	.2375	Sperm Candles	.52
Rio Coffee, Roasted	.296	Toilet Soap, BWI	.125
Rio Coffee, R. and G.	.27	Toilet Soap, Honey	.1325
Tea	.70	Toilet Soap, Lye	.16
Sugar, brown	.1425	Toilet Soap	.18
Vinegar	.27	Table Salt	.025
Candles	.085	Cayenne Pepper	.75
Soap	.075	Mackerel	.14
Salt	.015	White Fish	.105
Pepper, blk	.39	Cod	.0775
Desiccated Potatoes	.11	Halibut	.12
Desiccated Mixed Vegs.	.22	Herring	.118
Tobacco	.078	Sardines	.1925
Onions	.0475	Salmon	.65
Hops	.45	Dried Apples	.085
B. Bacon	.215	Dried Peaches	.15
Ham	.18	Raisins	.255
Smoked Beef	.15	Prunes	.15
Cucumber Pickles	.60	Allspice	.58
Onion Pickles	.70	Cinnamon	.97

Fine Pickles	3.20	Cloves	.72
Oysters, Canned	.18	Ginger	.46
Clams, Canned	.30	Nutmeg	1.40
Lobsters, Canned	.15	Lemon Extract, Bottle	.20
Tomatoes	.125	Vanilla Extract, Bottle	.295
Green Corn	.25	Worcestershire Sauce	.80
Green Peas	.23	Corn Starch, lb.	.13
Lima Beans	.36	Farina	.14
String Beans	.145	Tapioca	.20
Potatoes	.25	Maizena	.12
Onions	.30	Chocolate	.41
Peaches	.25	Vermicelli	.29
Pears	.25	Macaroni	.27
Fine Apples	.2925	Yeast Powder, box	.1875
Cranberry Sauce	.38	Salaratus	.15
Currant Jelly	.48	Bicarbonate Soda	.15
P. A. Jelly	.48	Cream Tartar	.38
Assorted Jams	.54	Lard	.19
Raspberry Jam	.525	Fac. Cheese	.35
Blackberry Jam	.4167	P. A.	.28
Strawberry Jam	.5433	Sperm Oil	2.405
Assorted Preserves	.59	Lard Oil	1.4
Quince Preserves	.5875	Laundry Starch	.1125
P. A. Preserves	.58	Laundry Indigo	1.75
Peach Preserves	.5533	Asparagus	.4167
Pear Preserves	.59	Wicking, L.	.75
Strawberry Preserves	.5625	Wicking, M.	.50
Milk	.2875	Wicking, S.	.30
Mustard	.85	Wicking, B.	1.20

Fort Harker was a supply depot for the Hancock Expedition and military posts farther west during 1867. The list of 195 escorts and other field assignments provides an indication of the activities of the quartermaster department and other departments, and it shows how busy the troops in garrison were. In addition to these duties, troops were engaged in constructing new buildings at the post, standing guard duty, performing fatigue duty, and doing everything else required to maintain the post. Abbreviations: NCO = noncommissioned officer; men = privates; Co. = Company; Lt. = Lieutenant; RR = railroad. Notes: W. W. Wright was chief engineer, Union Pacific Railroad, Eastern Division: General A. J. Smith was commander of the District of the Upper Arkansas; Colonel Elmer Otis was inspector general for the military district; General W. S. Hancock was commander of the Department of the Missouri; Thomas Murphy was superintendent of Indian affairs for the central superintendency; Major Henry Inman was depot quartermaster at Fort Harker. In 1868, by comparison, there were only thirty-nine such assignments. The supply depot was closed in 1869.

Date	Escort & Assignment
April 20, 18	NCO & 10 men, escort government train to Fort Hays
April 23, 1867	Co. A, 10th Cav., escort government train to Fort Larned
April 23, 1867	NCO & 5 men, escort government train to Fort Hays
April 25, 1867	NCO & recruits at post, escort government train to Fort Hays
April 27, 1867	NCO & 10 men, escort government train to Fort Larned
April 27, 1867	NCO & 10 men, escort government train to Fort Hays
April 28, 1867	NCO & 10 men, escort government train to Fort Hays
May 2, 1867	NCO & 10 men, escort government train to Fort Hay
May 6, 1867	Lt. & detachment of recruits, escort train to Fort Hays
May 8, 1867	NCO & 10 men, escort train to Fort Hays
May 13, 1867	NCO & 6 men, escort paymaster to Fort Hays
May 15, 1867	NCO & 5 men, escort government train to Fort Hays
May 16, 1867	NCO & 6 men, escort Gen. A. J. Smith to Fort Hays
May 22, 1867	NCO & 20 men, escort government train to Fort Hays
May 22, 1867	NCO & 15 men, escort government train to Fort Larned
May 24, 1867	NCO & 20 men, escort government train to Fort Larned
May 26, 1867	NCO & 5 men, escort train to Fort Hays
May 27, 1867	NCO & 10 men, escort government train to Fort Hays
May 27, 1867	NCO & 4 men, escort Santa Fe Mail Coach to Fort Larned

May 28, 1867	NCO & 5 men, escort paymaster to Salina
May 28, 1867	NCO & 5 men, escort government train to Fort Hays
May 29, 1867	NCO & 15 men, escort government train to Fort Hays
May 29, 1867	NCO & 3 men, escort an officer to Fort Larned
May 31, 1867	NCO & 15 men, escort government train to Fort Hays
June 1, 1867	NCO & 5 men, escort government train to Fort Hays
June 2, 1867	NCO & 5 men, escort government train to Fort Hays
June 4, 1867	NCO & 10 men, escort government train to Fort Dodge
June 6, 1867	NCO & 10 men, escort government train to Fort Hays
June 6, 1867	Lt. & Co. E, 17th Inf., escort Gen. W. S. Hancock to Fort Hays
June 8, 1867	NCO & 10 men, escort government train to Fort Hays
June 11, 1867	NCO & 10 men, escort beef cattle herd to Fort Hays
June 11, 1867	NCO & 10 men, escort W. W. Wright to Fort Hays
June 20, 1867	NCO & 10 men, escort government train to Fort Larned
June 20, 1867	NCO & 15 men, escort government trains to Fort Hays
June 21, 1867	NCO & 10 men, escort Santa Fe Mail Coach to Fort Zarah
June 25, 1867	2 NCOs & 10 men, escort RR survey party at Wilson's Creek
June 26, 1867	NCO & 10 men, encamp on bluffs above Ellsworth for 2 days
June 26, 1867	NCO & 10 men, escort Santa Fe Mail Coach to Fort Zarah
June 26, 1867	NCO & 10 men, escort train to Fort Hays
June 27, 1867	NCO & 10 men, escort train to Camp on Little Arkansas
June 27, 1867	NCO & 10 men, guard at Sternberg farm, 2 miles from Post
June 28, 1867	5 men sent to join detachment at Wilson's Creek
June 29, 1867	NCO & 15 men, escort Colonel Elmer Otis to Fort Zarah
June 30, 1867	NCO & 10 men, relieve guard at Sternberg farm
July 4, 1867	NCO & 20 men, escort train of government stores to Fort Hays
July 5, 1867	NCO & 10 men, escort Santa Fe Mail Coach to Plum Creek
July 5, 1867	NCO & 10 men, relieve guard at Sternberg farm
July 5, 1867	NCO & 15 men, escort train of govt. stores to Fort Larned
July 6, 1867	NCO & 10 men, join guard at Sternberg farm
July 7, 1867	NCO & 20 men, escort train of govt. forage to Fort Hays
July 7, 1867	NCO & 20 men, escort government train to Fort Hays
July 8, 1867	NCO & 20 men, escort government train to Fort Larned
July 8, 1867	NCO & 10 men, escort train to Fort Hays
July 10, 1867	NCO & 15 men, escort government train to Fort Hays
July 11, 1867	NCO & 15 men, escort government train to Fort Larned
July 12, 1867	NCO & 15 men, relieve detachment at Wilson's Creek

July 13, 1867	NCO & 10 men, escort train to Fort Larned
July 14, 1867	NCO & 10 men, escort Santa Fe Mail Coach to Plum Creek
July 16, 1867	NCO & 10 men, escort government train to Fort Larned
July 16, 1867	NCO & 5 men, escort detachment from Wilson's Creek to Post
July 16, 1867	NCO & 10 men, escort government train to Fort Hays
July 21, 1867	NCO & 15 men, escort government train to Fort Wallace
July 21, 1867	NCO & 5 men, escort Overland Mail to Big Creek Station
July 21, 1867	NCO & 15 men, escort Santa Fe Mail Coach to Plum Creek
July 23, 1867	NCO & 10 men, escort Santa Fe Mail Coach to Plum Creek
July 25, 1867	NCO & 10 men, escort government train to Fort Larned
July 25, 1867	NCO & 5 men, escort Santa Fe Mail Coach to Plum Creek
July 26, 1867	NCO & 5 men, escort Overland Mail to Big Creek Station
July 26, 1867	NCO & 10 men, escort govt. train to mouth of Little Arkansas
July 27, 1867	NCO & 9 men, escort government train to Fort Larned
July 27, 1867	NCO & 10 men, guard Plum Creek Station
July 28, 1867	2 men, escort to Wilson's Creek [who or what not stated]
July 28, 1867	NCO & 3 men, escort Overland Mail to Big Creek Station
July 28, 1867	NCO & 10 men, escort Santa Fe Mail Coach to Plum Creek
July 30, 1867	NCO & 15 men, escort General William Hoffman
July 30, 1867	3 NCOs & 30 men, escort ammunition train to Fort Wallace
July 31, 1867	NCO & 8 men, escort Santa Fe Mail Coach to Plum Creek
August 2, 1867	NCO & 10 men, escort government train to Fort Zarah
August 3, 1867	NCO & 10 men, escort government train to Fort Dodge
August 4, 1867	NCO & 8 men, escort Santa Fe Mail Coach to Plum Creek
August 6, 1867	NCO & 8 men, escort Santa Fe Mail Coach to Plum Creek
August 8, 1867	2 NCOs & 25 men, escort train to Fort Dodge
August 8, 1867	NCO & 8 men, escort Santa Fe Mail Coach to Plum Creek
August 9, 1867	NCO & 10 men, escort train to Fort Larned
August 10, 1867	NCO & 5 men, escort train to Fort Hays
August 11, 1867	NCO & 10 men, escort train to Fort Hays
August 11, 1867	NCO & 10 men, escort government train to Fort Zarah
August 11, 1867	NCO & 5 men, escort Santa Fe Mail Coach to Plum Creek
August 13, 1867	3 NCOs & 33 men, escort train to Fort Wallace
August 14, 1867	NCO & 5 men, escort Santa Fe Mail Coach to Plum Creek
August 14, 1867	NCO & 9 men, escort trains to Fort Larned
August 15, 1867	NCO & 5 men, escort Santa Fe Mail Coach to Plum Creek
August 16, 1867	3 NCOs & 17 men, escort train to Fort Wallace

August 18, 1867	NCO & 4 men, escort train to Fort Zarah
August 18, 1867	NCO & 4 men, escort train to Fort Larned
August 18, 1867	NCO & 6 men, escort Santa Fe Mail Coach to Plum Creek
August 20, 1867	NCO & 4 men, escort wagon load of supplies to Plum Creek
August 20, 1867	NCO & 10 men, escort train to Fort Larned
August 20, 1867	NCO & 12 men, escort train to Fort Hays
August 20, 1867	NCO & 5 men, escort Santa Fe Mail Coach to Plum Creek
August 21, 1867	NCO & 10 men, escort train to Fort Larned
August 22, 1867	NCO & 9 men, escort train to Fort Hays
August 22, 1867	NCO & 5 men, escort Santa Fe Mail Coach to Plum Creek
August 22, 1867	NCO & 5 men, escort government train to Fort Hays
August 23, 1867	Detachment of recruits (46), escort train to Fort Larned
August 24, 1867	NCO & 9 men, escort train to Downer's Station
August 24, 1867	Detachment of recruits (46), escort train to Fort Dodge
August 24, 1867	2 NCOs & 23 men, escort Gen. Hancock to end of railroad
August 25, 1867	NCO & 16 men, escort train to Fort Larned
August 26, 1867	NCO & 5 men, escort Santa Fe Mail Coach to Plum Creek
August 26, 1867	NCO & 9 men, escort train to Fort Hays
August 27, 1867	NCO & 9 men, assist civil authorities to arrest criminals
August 27, 1867	NCO & 5 men, escort Santa Fe Mail Coach to Plum Creek
August 27, 1867	NCO & 22 men, escort surveying party
August 27, 1867	Lt. & detachment of recruits, escort train to Fort Lyon
August 28, 1867	NCO & 5 men, escort Thomas Murphy to Ellsworth
August 29, 1867	NCO & 19 men, escort train to Downer's Station
August 29, 1867	NCO & 5 men, escort Santa Fe Mail Coach to Plum Creek
August 30, 1867	NCO & 6 men, escort train to Fort Hays
August 30, 1867	NCO & 10 men, escort train to Fort Dodge
September 1, 1867	NCO & 10 men, escort train to Fort Dodge
September 2, 1867	NCO & 4 men, escort train to Fort Dodge
September 2, 1867	NCO & 4 men, escort Santa Fe Mail Coach to Plum Creek
September 2, 1867	NCO & 10 men, relieve detachment at Plum Creek Station
September 3, 1867	NCO & 4 men, escort train to Fort Hays
September 3, 1867	NCO & 4 men, escort Santa Fe Mail Coach to Plum Creek
September 4, 1867	NCO & 6 men, escort train to Fort Larned
September 4, 1867	NCO & 5 men, escort train to Fort Zarah
September 4, 1867	NCO & 10 men, escort Captain A. F. Rockwell to Fort Larned
September 4, 1867	2 NCOs & 7 men, escort train to Fort Hays

September 4, 1867	NCO & 3 men, escort for Gen. Horace Brooks
September 5, 1867	NCO & 15 men, escort train to Fort Wallace
September 5, 1867	NCO & 4 men, escort Santa Fe Mail Coach to Plum Creek
September 6, 1867	NCO & 4 men, escort train to Fort Larned
September 7, 1867	NCO & 4 men, sent to Ellsworth to apprehend deserter
September 7, 1867	NCO & 10 men, escort train to Fort Wallace
September 8, 1867	NCO & 14 men, escort Santa Fe Mail Coach to Plum Creek
September 9, 1867	NCO & 6 men, escort train to Fort Larned
September 10, 1867	2 NCOs & 12 men, guard at Wilson's Creek
September 11, 1867	NCO & 5 men, escort train to Fort Larned
September 11, 1867	NCO & 5 men, escort Mr. Butterfield to Fort Larned
September 11, 1867	NCO & 5 men, escort ox train to Fort Dodge
September 12, 1867	NCO & 10 men, escort train to Fort Larned
September 13, 1867	NCO & 4 men, escort Santa Fe Mail Coach to Plum Creek
September 14, 1867	NCO & 15 men, escort train to Fort Larned
September 15, 1867	NCO & 4 men, escort Santa Fe Mail Coach to Plum Creek
September 15, 1867	4 NCOs & 6 men, escort train to Fort Larned
September 16, 1867	NCO & 4 men, escort Santa Fe Mail Coach to Plum Creek
September 16, 1867	NCO & 10 men, escort survey officer to Fort Larned
September 18, 1867	NCO & 5 men, escort Santa Fe Mail Coach to Plum Creek
September 18, 1867	NCO & 10 men, escort duty [where not given]
September 19, 1867	NCO & 14 men, escort mule train to Fort Larned
September 19, 1867	NCO & 5 men, escort ox train to Fort Larned
September 19, 1867	NCO & 5 men, escort Major M. H. Kidd to Cow Creek
September 20, 1867	NCO & 4 men, escort Santa Fe Mail Coach to Plum Creek
September 20, 1867	NCO & 10 men, escort train to Fort Hays
September 21, 1867	NCO & 8 men, escort train to Fort Dodge
September 22, 1867	NCO & 4 men, escort Santa Fe Mail Coach to Plum Creek
September 23, 1867	3 NCOs & 22 men, escort government train to Fort Hays
September 24, 1867	NCO & 4 men, escort Santa Fe Mail Coach to Plum Creek
September 26, 1867	NCO & 10 men, escort government train to Downer's Station
September 26, 1867	NCO & 4 men, escort Santa Fe Mail Coach to Plum Creek
September 26, 1867	NCO & 5 men, escort train to Monument Station
September 27, 1867	NCO & 10 men, escort herd of horses to end of railroad
September 28, 1867	NCO & 14 men, escort government mule train to Fort Larned
September 29, 1867	NCO & 4 men, escort Santa Fe Mail Coach to Plum Creek
September 29, 1867	NCO & 15 men, escort government train to Fort Hays

October 1, 1867	NCO & 4 men, escort Santa Fe Mail Coach to Plum Creek
October 4, 1867	NCO & 10 men, escort government train to Fort Dodge
October 6, 1867	NCO & 4 men, escort Santa Fe Mail Coach to Plum Creek
October 6, 1867	NCO & 6 men, escort government train to Fort Larned
October 8, 1867	NCO & 8 men, escort duty [where not given]
October 9, 1867	NCO & 10 men, escort government train to Fort Larned
October 9, 1867	NCO & 10 men, relieve detachment at Plum Creek Station
October 10, 1867	NCO & 4 men, escort Santa Fe Mail Coach to Plum Creek
October 10, 1867	NCO & 5 men, escort train to Fort Larned
October 11, 1867	2 NCOs & 18 men, escort train to Fort Wallace
October 11, 1867	NCO & 6 men, escort train to Fort Larned
October 12, 1867	NCO & 6 men, escort train to Fort Larned
October 14, 1867	NCO & 10 men, escort government train to Monument Station
October 14, 1867	NCO & 4 men, escort Santa Fe Mail Coach to Plum Creek
October 16, 1867	NCO & 10 men, escort mule train to Fort Larned
October 17, 1867	NCO & 10 men, escort trains to Fort Wallace
October 20, 1867	NCO & 4 men, escort Santa Fe Mail Coach to Plum Creek
October 24, 1867	NCO & 4 men, escort Santa Fe Mail Coach to Plum Creek
October 25, 1867	NCO & 10 men, escort train to Fort Wallace
October 29, 1867	NCO & 4 men, escort Santa Fe Mail Coach to Plum Creek
October 29, 1867	NCO & 6 men, escort train to Downer's Station
October 29, 1867	NCO & 4 men, escort train to Fort Zarah
October 31, 1867	NCO & 15 men, escort surveying party
November 5, 1867	NCO & 15 men, escort Major Henry Inman
November 5, 1867	NCO & 10 men, relieve guard at Plum Creek Station
November 18, 1867	NCO & 2 men, escort paymaster to Fort Hays
November 30, 1867	NCO & 1 man, courier duty between Forts Harker & Larned
December 1, 1867	NCO & 10 men, escort paymaster

Carriker, Robert C. and Eleanor R. Carriker. *An Army Wife on the Frontier: The Memoirs of Alice Blackwood Baldwin, 1867–1877*. Salt Lake City: University of Utah Library, 1975.

Keim, De Benneville Randolph. *Sheridan's Troopers on the Borders: A Winter Campaign on the Plains*. Glorieta, N.M.: Rio Grande Press, 1977.

Kennedy, W. J. D. *On the Plains with Custer and Hancock: The Journal of Isaac Coates, Army Surgeon*. Boulder, Colo.: Johnson Books, 1997.

Leckie, William H. *The Military Conquest of the Southern Plains*. Norman: University of Oklahoma Press, 1963.

Rickey, Don. *Forty Miles a Day on Beans and Hay: The Enlisted Soldier Fighting the Indian Wars*. Norman: University of Oklahoma Press, 1963.

Rogers, Katherine. *The Sternberg Fossil Hunters: A Dinosaur Dynasty*. Missoula: Montana Press Publishing Co., 1991.

Stallard, Patricia Y. *Glittering Misery: Dependents on the Indian Fighting Army*. Norman: University of Oklahoma Press, 1992.

Stanley, Henry M. *My Early Travels and Adventures in America*. Lincoln: University of Nebraska Press, 1982.

Utley, Robert M. *Frontier Regulars: The United States Army and the Indian, 1866–1891*. New York: Macmillan Publishing Co., 1973.

Utley, Robert M., ed. *Life in Custer's Cavalry: Diaries and Letters of Albert and Jennie Barnitz, 1867–1868*. New Haven: Yale University Press, 1977.

Acknowledgments

My thanks to the following individuals for their help, information, and encouragement in the preparation of this history: William Y. Chalfant, Virgil Dean, George Elmore, Marsha King, and Timothy A. Zwink. The assistance and courtesy of the personnel at the following institutions was invaluable and is gratefully acknowledged: National Archives, U. S. Army Military History Institute, and Kansas State Historical Society. My wife, Bonita, assisted with the research and assumed extra responsibilities so I could devote time to this project.

Illustration Credits

This publication has been financed in part with federal funds from the National Park Service, a division of the United States Department of the Interior, and administered by the Kansas State Historical Society. The contents and opinions, however, do not necessarily reflect the views or policies of the United States Department of the Interior or the Kansas State Historical Society.

The program receives federal financial assistance. Under Title VI of the Civil Rights Act of 1964, Section 504 of the Rehabilitation Act of 1973, and the Age Discrimination Act of 1975, as amended, the United States Department of the Interior prohibits discrimination on the basis of race, color, national origin, disability, or age in its federally assisted programs. If you believe you have been discriminated against in any program, activity, or facility as described above, or if you desire further information, please write to: Office of Equal Opportunity, National Park Service, P.O. Box 37127, Washington, D.C. 20012-7127.